Believing

Reflections of Faith

MICHAEL MISIAK

Michael Misiak

Printed in the United States of America

Print ISBN: 978-1-54395-863-8

eBook ISBN: 978-1-54395-864-5

CONTENTS

Prologue

In my first book— *God Loves You and I'm Trying!*— I kept the stories short and in true form to the magazine *Reader's Digest,* which is often found in the bathroom library. In fact, one reader commented that my book was, indeed, the bathroom companion to spirituality. It was a moment of great pride, knowing that not only were people reading my book, but the book actually held a great secondary purpose in its placement, much like the Sears & Roebuck catalog in rural America.

I promise in the latter part of this book to hold true to the short vignette form of storytelling, but in the first part of this book, I wish to elaborate more on the essential elements of my faith. This book's beginning will ask you to test your belief system as it relates to God, the Bible, Jesus, and the human soul.

As one friend and nonbeliever pointed out to me, I may be completely delusional. Fair enough, but I told him that I am no more or less delusional in believing than he is in not believing. We often believe what we want to, and not often enough, what we need to.

My quest for God has been lifelong, from childhood, and will continue past my final breath. Please know that I claim no authority as an acclaimed theologian, but I am an expert in what I believe. This is my journey, and I invite you along.

Introduction

It has been said of God: "For those who believe, no proof is required. For those who do not believe, no proof is sufficient." This speaks to two places in human thinking, a black or white, yay or nay, belief or disbelief, but not of the gray area of seeking and wondering.

It stretches the boundaries of human reasoning to make an attempt to even fathom the concept of an infinite being when we exist in a finite world. It was a stretch for those living just 200 years ago to imagine flying from one coast to the other in just hours, or a telephone, or FaceTime. Think of the medical miracles and advancements that at one time were unimaginable. We live and enjoy the fruits of the imagination of those who came before us, those who stretched their thinking and boldly said, "Way!" when others said, "No way!"

Yet in this stretching, this glorious seeking of knowledge and advancement of the human race, have we become so confident to say that there is no God? Some have, and support their beliefs with science, or so they declare.

As a society, we tend to boast of our intelligence, justified in the wondrous advancements in technology. Just because our gadgetry has become more sophisticated doesn't necessarily mean we as humanity have grown. We suffer from what is called *chronological snobbery*. We puff up our egos by fooling ourselves that we are so together and so smart, and thinking those ancients just didn't know any better. Nothing could be further from the truth.

There were brilliant teachers and philosophers, artists and musicians, men and women of science, all who existed long before the advent of high-definition television. If you really believe that we are more civil and intelligent than past generations, watch a few reruns of the Jerry Springer show or some of the foolish stunts posted on YouTube, and you may agree with me that there should have been more chlorine in the gene pool. Brilliant people, and not so brilliant people, have always been on the planet, and now we can watch them all on our phones and in our media rooms.

If you are reading this from a place grounded in faith, let this be a reaffirmation that God is real. If you are reading this with no belief, or disbelief, open your mind and heart to at least entertain the possibility of the reality of God.

There are two ways to approach accepting or rejecting information. One is called convergent thinking. Convergent thinking is the process of searching out data and information that will best support and lead to a preconceived idea. The second one is called divergent thinking. Divergent thinking is open to seeing all possibilities and accepting that there may be more than one solution or end. Both are important to our understanding.

I suspect we've all encountered a friend, coworker, or even family member who is immovable in their thinking and opinion about someone or something. No matter how you counter with facts or evidence to the contrary, they only listen to that which supports their preconceived opinion. That is convergent thinking.

And so I ask you to be a divergent thinker. As you read, open your mind and heart to the possibilities that I present and believe. Don't dig in your heels. Don't put up the shields. Just give it thought, some consideration, with an open mind, and most important, an open heart. This is a world of possibilities, of promise, and of hope. Who wouldn't want more of that in their life?

What I'm going to present to you may seem counterintuitive and countercultural, and in many cases it is. It may go against the grain of who and what you perceive you are. Please roll with it and push through the angst. No pain, no gain.

Together we will just be scratching the surface of a spiritual dig that runs deep. There are deeper studies of the character of God that go beyond the theme of this book. I leave that to the Calvins and Spurgeons and Bonhoeffers of the world, brilliant theologians of deep faith and thinking. There is a buffet of knowledge and resources readily available when you're hungry for the next step. My hope is to just bring you to the lunchroom.

Believing the Unbelievable

There are things on earth that defy explanation. Our senses can't grasp them. Science can't explain them. Case in point is the story of the Church of Our Lady of the Assumption in Hiroshima, Japan.

World War II. After six months of intense firebombing of 67 Japanese cities, the Empire of Japan still refused to surrender. President Harry S. Truman gave the executive order to use the most horrific weapon of war created at that time, the atomic bomb. The goal of the weapon was to convince Japan to surrender unconditionally.

On August 6, 1945, the nuclear weapon named *Little Boy* was dropped from a B-29 bomber named *Enola Gay* on the city of Hiroshima. People were vaporized instantly. Everything within a one-mile radius was completely destroyed. Buildings as far away as nine miles from the epicenter collapsed. The radiation generated by the blast was so strong that people miles away would die within a few days.

This history is painful, but I'm driving towards an amazing point that is unexplainable. In the midst of this carnage, just eight blocks from ground zero, about a half of a mile, a two-story Catholic presbytery remained intact, and the eight German Jesuit priests were all found with only minor injuries.

Dr. Stephen A. Rinehart, a physicist with the U.S. Department of Defense, studied the incident, and concluded that there are no physical laws to explain why the Jesuits were untouched, given their proximity to the blast. The amount of radiation alone should have killed them in minutes. He wrote:

> Their residence should still have been utterly destroyed (temp; 2000° F and air blast pressures; 100 psi). In contrast, unreinforced masonry or brick walls (representative of commercial construction) are destroyed at 3 psi, which will also cause car damage and burst windows. At 10 psi, a human will experience severe lung and heart damage, burst eardrums and at 20 psi your limbs can be blown off. Your head will be blown off by 40 psi and no residential or unreinforced commercial construction would be left standing. At 80 psi even reinforced concrete is heavily damaged and no human would be alive because your skull would be crushed. All the cotton clothes would be on fire at 350° F (probably at 275° F) and your lungs would be inoperative within a minute breathing air (even for a few seconds) at these temperatures.

Dr. Rinehart went on to conclude that there was some other (external) force present ". . . whose power and/or capability to transform energy and matter as it relates to humans is beyond current comprehension." So in other words, there had to be a force, an energy, large enough to push back and cancel the weapon's effect.

All eight priests lived out their lives in full health with no radiation sickness and no loss of hearing. Father Hubert Shiffer, who headed the community, was examined and questioned by more than 200 scientists. They were unable to explain how he and his companions had survived.

Believers in God would, without hesitation, call this a miracle. There are hundreds of stories of miracle healings that defy medical explanation. There are countless stories of people walking away unscathed from horrific automobile accidents. Each story challenges our daily and usual reasoning, and stretches the mind to the possibility of the unbelievable.

The great thinkers in our culture, the inventors, the scientists, the philosophers, are successful and called great because they think outside the box. They think outside and beyond the boxes of laws, rules, and traditions that regulate customary and accepted thinking.

Be a great thinker. Open your mind and, most importantly, open your heart to the possibility of the impossible, the sanity inside the crazy. There are things that at one time were unexplainable and now have explanations. There are things now proven that at one time had no proof. This happened only because of great thinkers. Great thinkers think for themselves. Be one!

Believing in the Soul

We've all heard and perhaps used the term "soul-searching." We know the meaning to be "examination of one's conscience especially with regard to motives and values." At least that's how Merriam-Webster defines it. Other thoughts on the matter include the words self-contemplation, observation, and reflection. In simple terms, soul-searching is a time-out. It's time set aside to pause and think.

Now it seems to me you don't have to believe that you have a soul to do soul-searching. The phrase is universally diluted to mean taking an inventory of character rather than something spiritual, something involving psychology, the human condition, and the culmination of human experiences. Besides, do we really have a soul, and if so, what is it?

The skeptic will say that belief in the soul is man's lame attempt to justify an existence that ends with the final breath, that we have a psychological need to validate and find comfort in a life lived, and that we are fooling ourselves into happiness. Well, they've got me there, because I'm pretty darn happy believing that the essence of who I am is eternal and will always be connected to the one who created me.

I cannot honestly say when I knew that I had a soul, but as early as five years old, I believed in God, as far as a five-year-old can believe. I was raised Russian Orthodox with two guaranteed visits to church on

Christmas and Easter and a random visit between holidays. Despite the infrequency of our church attendance, as a family we would say nightly prayers before my bedtime, so I was infused with a belief in God. Beyond that, and a checklist of dos and don'ts starting with the Ten Commandments mixed with Misiak family morals, I was on my own in the quest and the questions.

As with most children of a single-digit age, my sleep set the stage for dreams, but also for non-dreams—happenings that my parents would reassure me were only dreams, but I knew different. I remember to this day the sensation of standing on my front porch steps and slowly rising into the air. Of course my body was still in bed, which some would say is evidence that I was dreaming, but this was no dream.

As years passed, my soul searching became a soul excavation, digging deeper than just superficial beliefs. I read books both within and outside the Christian realm that described the infinite soul. There are amazing accounts of people dying and their soul, their essence, leaving their body and going to another dimension, another world.

Again the skeptic might interject that these near-death experiences, these out-of-body tales, are nothing more than the brain manufacturing a dream or delusion as it shuts down. They may even point to the specific part of the brain that can produce such an experience. Such was the case of Dr. Eben Alexander, a distinguished neurosurgeon at Children's Hospitals and Harvard Medical School in Boston.

In his book *Proof of Heaven*, Dr. Alexander tells the story of how he believed that near-death experiences might feel real, but were simply fantasies produced by the brain under extreme stress. He held this belief until he regained consciousness after being in a coma for seven days due to a rare disease.

While in the coma, the parts of his brain that control thoughts and emotions, the very things that make us human, had shut down completely, flatlined, and yet when he awoke, he told the story of leaving his body and journeying beyond this world into the "deepest realms of super-physical existence".

"Before he underwent his journey, he could not reconcile his knowledge of neuroscience with any belief in heaven, God, or the soul. Today Alexander is a doctor who believes that true health can be achieved only when we realize that God and the soul are real and that death is not the end of personal existence but only a transition" (Taken from the book jacket.)

Let me take a moment to share a bit of history to set the stage for this next point. Dr. Alexander was adopted and separated from his birth family. His birth mother was only sixteen years old when she agreed to give him up for adoption in 1954.

In 2000 he found out that his birth parents did get married, and had three more children, two daughters and a son. Unfortunately, one daughter died two years previous. The family was still grieving and couldn't face meeting the son they gave up for adoption. Finally, in 2007, Dr. Alexander met his birth parents and his biological siblings.

It was in November of 2008, while Dr. Alexander was in a coma, that his soul, his essence, his true self, left his physical body and went to a place of light and love. He was guided by a beautiful woman the whole time. It wasn't until after awakening from his coma that he realized who she was.

When he was out of the hospital for just four months, his biological sister sent a picture of the other sister who died, the one he never met. It was her—the angelic being who greeted him, comforted him, and guided him while he was out of his body.

An older artifact of evidence in my soul excavation came to me in 1975 in the book *Life After Life* by another doctor, Dr. Raymond Moody. During the early 1970s, Dr. Moody studied more than one hundred subjects who had experienced clinical death and been revived. The stories of their out-of-body experiences have striking similarities in spite of religious or social background differences. Many of the patients shared the experience of seeing their body surrounded by the medical team attempting to resuscitate them.

Once revived and able to speak, to the astonishment of the attending medical staff, those who were for a time out of their bodies could give specific facts as to the conversations of those in the room. They could describe in detail what everyone was doing in that room, as well as what loved ones were doing in the waiting room.

There were shared stories of being greeted by deceased loved ones, and being told that it wasn't "their time" and that they must go back. All of the accounts had a common thread that there was nothing to fear in dying, for their being, their soul, will go on. One person said that the body is more like a prison, and when it's time to leave it behind, you are truly free.

Can the soul leave a body that is not dying? Is it possible to actually control an out-of-body experience? Digging deeper and going further back in years are the writings of Edgar Cayce, who before his death in 1945 had thousands of out-of-body experiences into the afterlife. He was a wonder to the medical community because of his ability to diagnose and specify a treatment for gravely ill people, often hundreds of miles away, through his out-of-body experiences.

There is documented evidence at the Edgar Cayce's Association for Research and Enlightenment (ARE) in Virginia Beach, Virginia.

Rolling back the clock even further and beyond our twentieth-century American culture, we find great similarities in the Tibetan Book of the Dead. The book, estimated to have been written in the eighth century, is a compilation of the teachings of sages over many centuries. It describes the soul leaving the body into a new world with a new body, which they call the "shining body," a body not of physical material substance. This body is not subject to physical laws and can move through walls and mountains. It may meet other beings in the same type of shining bodies. The book also speaks of meeting "pure light."

Four hundred years before the birth of Jesus, the Greek philosopher Plato believed and wrote of the existence of a soul separate from the physical body, and that the physical body was only a temporary vehicle for the soul. In his writings, he discusses how the soul, when separated from the body, may meet other souls in other realms beyond the physical world. Plato thought that being born into the physical world and body is really a loss of the pure and full awareness of the consciousness of the soul. If birth was a loss, than Plato described death more as an awakening and clarity of being.

Turning back time before Plato, we know through hieroglyphics that the ancient Egyptians believed that humans had a life force, which left the body at death. Thousands of years before the birth of Christ, mankind believed in the hope of life eternal, which now brings me to my final source, the Bible.

The Bible clearly states that we humans are eternal souls living for a short time in a body that will die. Time and time again there is a direct and clear distinction between the body and the soul.

Matthew 10:28 says, "And do not fear those who kill the body but cannot kill the soul. Rather fear him who can destroy both soul and body in hell."

1 Thessalonians 5:23 repeats a distinction of body and soul: "Now may the God of peace himself sanctify you completely, and may your whole spirit and soul and body be kept blameless at the coming of our Lord Jesus Christ."

1 Corinthians 15:42–44 says, "So is it with resurrection of the dead. What is sown is perishable; what is raised is imperishable. It is sown in dishonor; it is raised in glory. It is sown in weakness; it is raised in power. It is sown a natural body; it is raised a spiritual body. If there is a natural body, there is also a spiritual body."

I now ask the skeptic if it is logical to dismiss the testimonies and beliefs of millions of people over thousands of years as fantasy. Is this just a case of mass hysteria or delusion, or is it possible that you indeed have a soul? Can it be that we are truly spiritual beings piloting physical bodies for a short time before going back to the spiritual realm?

We shouldn't dismiss the eyewitness testimony of people like Alexander, Moody, and Cayce. In today's court of law, eyewitness testimony is admissible as evidence. Evidence is submitted to prove a case in a trial, and the trial is held to get to the truth. Truth is your ultimate freedom. Keep an open mind and an open heart, and judge for yourself. Time to do some soul-searching.

Believing the Bible

To understand the Christian story is to know how this belief has survived over two thousand years. Tradition plays a part in sustaining the faith handed down and spoken of from generation to generation. Where you were born and the family you were born into usually cultivates your belief or nonbelief in God and how to approach him.

The major written source of the Christian legacy is, of course, the Bible. Now I know that someone reading this is thinking, "How can a book written thousands of years ago still tell the original truth of what happened when it has been translated over all of these years by men? What about human error? And who's to say it isn't just an elaborate story written to either give people false hope or to control them. I mean, come on, the church after all is a business!"

I know someone reading this is thinking this, because truth be told, I thought it once. The Bible was confusing to me, with a whole bunch of Jewish genealogy and a litany of who begot who begot who. Reading the Old Testament without someone to mentor you can derail your quest. At least it did for me. It went cross grain to what I thought was logical. I earnestly wanted to believe that the Bible was true, but just didn't understand it.

That was before I joined a great Bible-based church that unpacked this amazing book. That was before I actually did some digging on my own, looking into the history and backstory of the Bible. I believe with great assurance that this book is the real deal, having survived the ages, and I hope that by the end of this chapter, you will lean closer to that camp of thinking.

Our starting place is what is the Bible? The word *bible* comes from the Greek word "biblia" or books. It is divided into two larger sections called the Old Testament and the New Testament. The Old Testament refers to everything that led up to the time of Jesus. The New Testament speaks of the time of Jesus from his birth to the resurrection and into the revelation of things to come.

The Bible was written by men who were inspired by God. Now let's unpack that a bit. None of the men who wrote books of the Bible wrote for a living. Moses was a shepherd. John was a fisherman, Paul a tentmaker. Luke was a physician. David was a shepherd boy who would grow up to be king. It would have been unpredictable that with their given stations in life they would rise to such esteemed authorship, yet they wrote and preached with an authority and wisdom that they couldn't have learned or gained if not for an outside influence, which I believe was the inspiration of God through the Holy Spirit. How the actual writing process went down is a mystery to me.

Could this inspired writing have been a form of automatic writing, where they sat in a trance-like state, put their conscious minds to the side, and allowed an outside force (let's call it the Holy Spirit) to write through them? Or were visions and ideas revealed to them to write about using their unique human personality? Who's to say? It's not important to know for sure.

The overarching takeaway is that ordinary men wrote extraordinary writings that are, to this day, enriching lives with the promise of hope and peace. They wrote in the personality of who they were. Peter lived and wrote passionately. Paul was detail-orientated in life and in writing. John deeply loved the Lord and it showed in his writings. The important thing to know is that while written by different men in different times with different personalities, the scriptures are consistent in context and unwavering in the message.

You may be thinking that that's all well and good if you want to believe it, but where's the proof? Show me the evidence!

Let me plead my case by saying that none of the original manuscripts exist. (Not a great opening argument in any court of law.) Most of the writings were made on papyrus, which, because it is organic, decomposes over time. The good news is (did you catch what I did there . . . Good News) we have over 25,000 manuscripts that reconstruct and confirm the writings in the Bible we read today. There are 5,700 Greek manuscripts of the New Testament going back as far as AD 200. There are 10,000 Latin manuscripts. These writings show a uniform consistency across the centuries.

While papyrus is organic, some have survived the test of time. Papyrus 52, discovered in Egypt and dating back to AD 150, contains some of the writings of John's gospel, 70 years after John wrote it. Papyrus 66, found in 1952 near Dishna, Egypt, surprised scholars because the first 26 leaves were intact as was the stitching. It is one of the oldest well-preserved New Testament manuscripts containing much of John's writings.

The fact that any papyri have survived is a miracle, because they were written at a time of intense Christian persecution, and the burning of sacred Christian books was ordered by Emperor Diocletian in AD 303.

New archeological digs have unearthed more hard evidence to support the Bible record. The historical accuracy continues to be confirmed. The Soleb Temple dated 1396–1358 BC has the Egyptian inscription referencing the promised land of Canaan and a wandering "people of Yahweh," which coincides with the Bible's account of the Jewish people after their release from slavery in Egypt. The Mesha Stele or Moabite Stone was discovered in 1868 in Dibon in west-central Jordan. It dates back to King Mesha of Moab around 840 BC. The inscription parallels the history of King Mesha that is recorded in 2 Kings 3:4-27.

In January of 1947, the story goes that a shepherd noticed that some of his goats were climbing too high up in the cliffs 13 miles east of Jerusalem. He decided to climb the cliff face to bring them back. He unwittingly uncovered what is claimed to be one of the greatest archaeological discoveries of the twentieth century, the Dead Sea Scrolls.

Between 1947 and 1956, 11 caves were excavated to discover the remains of 825 to 870 separate scrolls, mostly on animal skins, some papyri, and one on copper. Fragments of every book of the Old Testament (Hebrew canon) have been discovered, except for the book of Esther.

Jerusalem is still a live archeological dig. In 2005, Dr. Eilat Mazar began her quest to find King David's palace. She found large walls that are described in 2 Samuel 5:11 for the building of a great house for King David. She also unearthed ancient seals used by court officials, and a variety of carved ivory utensils that would have only been used by royalty.

Across the street from the city of David, she has found more royal ruins that she claims belongs to King David's son, Solomon. In 2010, excavators found a giant wall that Dr. Mazar believes to be the city wall that is described in 1 Kings 3, which says, "He took Pharaoh's daughter and brought her into the city of David until he had finished building his own house and the house of the Lord and the wall around Jerusalem."

Pottery found at the ground floor was carbon dated to the tenth century BC, the time of Solomon. Jar handles were found with inscriptions that said, "To the king." There were large clay jars for storing grain, and on one was an inscription saying, "To the minister in charge of the bakery." A king would have a baker.

There are so many more interesting accounts of archeological evidence that are at your fingertips on the Internet. I have only presented a few to offer a baseline for belief.

If we can agree that manuscripts do exist written in the original Hebrew (Old Testament) and Greek (New Testament), then why are there so many translations of the Bible? The simpler answer is that language changes. Those who translated the Bible would write it in the language of the time so people could understand it. They would be diligent not to change Biblical doctrine, but would translate in such a way to make it understandable. Jesus spoke Aramaic. The New Testament was written in Greek. Not all words translate equally, but the story remains the same. The teachings stay original. Truth remains truth. In relatively recent times, we have dropped *thee, thou, and ye* from the King James Bible and translated them as *you, you,* and *you.* It doesn't distract from the meaning of the text. It helps the reading flow, being closer to the spoken language of the day. The changes in spelling and grammar were only intended to help the reader understand in the language of their time. No essential Christian beliefs and practices were impacted by these minor changes.

Let us now consider how the books were chosen to become the Bible, also called the canon of sacred scripture. Canon is taken from the Greek word which means "measuring rod." This is the standard of truth for judging what is to be the Christian life. There were religious writings that were counter to what the scriptures wrote, and so they didn't measure up to be included in the Bible.

There were some books that were accepted immediately and recognized as God's word. These were no-brainers in the decision process. Some were authored by eyewitnesses to the events they wrote about or directly taught to them by the apostles, the twelve closest disciples to Jesus. Another benchmark for inclusion of each book was the book's consistency with church practice and tradition. Was each book already being used by the church and accepted as the divine word of God? Some books were initially disputed because of the uncertainty of the authorship, but later acknowledged to be true. And some books were rejected immediately as false writings. It would be like including today's tabloid newspapers in history books.

The Protestant Bible that I read has 66 books. The Roman Catholic Bible has 73, having the addition of a collection of books called the Apocrypha. It was deemed to be part of the Catholic canon at the Council of Trent in 1546 and first published in the original King James Bible in 1611. The books remained positioned between the Old and New Testaments until they were removed in 1885. Protestant reformers like Martin Luther said, about these books, that they are not regarded as equal to the Holy Scriptures, and yet are profitable to read. Some argue that they never should have been removed. Some will argue that they should have never been included. The short of it is, the men who compiled the Bible did so with a great sense of responsibility to get it right.

What other book has proven to be timeless? Imagine going to a modern-day publisher and pitching a book you are coauthoring. You tell the publisher that it's going to take about 1,500 years to write and it will be penned by 40 authors, but the story line will be seamless, and it will be the most read book in the history of the world. Not only will it be the most read, but it will actually change the behavior of humanity.

I could only imagine that the publisher hearing this would politely smile and stall until his secretary could summon the police to get this insane person out of the office.

I belong to two men's prayer groups. We meet every Tuesday and Wednesday morning and study scripture and pray. We share preparing scripture lessons, and when I'm asked to lead, I'll do an Internet search for a particular topic that is on my heart, such as prayer or fear. I cut and paste all the scriptures into Word (great name for a software to organize Bible verses) and print them out to share. Without citing which book in the Bible they come from, I read aloud all the verses together at one time.

It's striking that no matter when the verses were written or by whom, they read as though they were penned by one hand. Both Old and New Testament verses, written hundreds of years apart, read as though one author penned them, and in essence, one author did.

You may still have your doubts, as you should. Reading what I have written should not evoke any grand epiphany. Your "aha" moment will only happen if you actually read the Bible for yourself. It will take time. Be patient, but deliberate. Remember, I was a doubter of the Bible who wanted to be without doubt. Until I studied the Bible and discussed it with fellow seekers, I was stalled in my spiritual growth. The Bible is often called the living word because it can speak to you and come to life the more that you study it. It's an adventure like no other.

Please open your heart to this. What *if* our creator gave us an owner's manual? Not just the short overview booklet like the one you might skim over when you buy a new car. I'm talking about that thick owner's manual that rests pristine underneath the napkins and hand sanitizer you keep in your glove compartment.

What *if* studying and reading this book calibrates your thinking, opens your heart, and grows your soul into a closer relationship to the life force of the universe? What *if* by reading this amazing book you become a better spouse, parent, coworker, and neighbor? What *if* you find new meaning and joy in life?

I don't see a down side to anything suggested here. I do see the need for commitment and a willingness to dig deep and work through the reading. I do see the absolute must of unpacking the Bible with fellow seekers and discussing and learning together.

But the greatest things I see in accepting the Bible are hope, faith, and love. I am a better man because of my Bible excavation. I thank God for the joy in the journey.

Believing in God

Who has seen the wind? We are all witnesses to the effects the wind has, the rustling of crisp leaves on a fall day, a kite sustained in flight, a spinnaker filled with wind propelling a sailboat.

Windmills provide energy. Wind chimes delight us in tubular evidence of an unseen hand. A gentle breeze cools us on a hot summer day, but who has *seen* the wind? Where does wind come from?

Science will explain that wind is the motion of air molecules caused by air and air pressure. Energy from the sun plays a role as it heats the earth unevenly, causing a difference in air pressure and causing wind. But who has *seen* the wind?

I dare say that there is not a living soul on earth who hasn't *felt* wind, but only a few would deep think its origin. Wind exists despite any disbelief.

Patients receiving radiation treatments can't see the high-energy particles or waves aimed at the cancer cells within them, but they believe they are real, sight unseen. We can't see the oxygen in the air we breathe, but we believe it's there with every breath we take. Left only to our physical senses, we could not believe many of the things that do exist are truly real.

Who has seen God? We are all witnesses to life events that are unexplainable by science or earthly logic. The unbeliever would call them luck or coincidences. The believer would call them miracles. The problem is that people want to sense God using the physical senses of the human body living in this material world, which is governed by natural laws. We want to define the indefinable. God is beyond total comprehension. Ask a third grader to define an algebra problem, and he will struggle with only a knowledge of the few numbers he recognizes. That doesn't negate the existence of algebra. It validates the limitations of understanding.

Is it wrong to define God? I would say only if your definition is finished. If you think you have all the answers, then you really have no answers. Our hunger to define should be more of a longing to be in a relationship with God.

To start to understand God, let's model the investigative technique of profiling that law enforcement officials implement during a manhunt. Let's build a profile of who we believe God to be based on the definition, descriptions, and eyewitness testimonies found in the Bible.

All throughout the Bible, God is described as an eternal being. I remember as a child asking my parents, "If God made everything, then who made God?" My parents' stock answer was that we were not meant to know some things, and that I would find out when I die, which wasn't very comforting and only led me to question more.

Even now the concept of something always being is hard to grasp. The concept of the big bang theory is not as far apart from the story of creation as some would have you believe. Biblically and scientifically, there was indeed one great moment of creation. My question for the big bangers is, what happened one second before the big bang, and what or who caused it? And where did the material come from to explode anyway?

How did an explosion create the intricacy and beauty of a flower petal, or a universe based on mathematics? The explosions I have seen in videos or photos show only carnage and disarray. I suppose it *is* possible for a hurricane to tear apart a house and reassemble it perfectly, but it hasn't happened yet, and is more improbable than probable.

Now, I don't want us to get paralyzed in this truly mind-blowing concept of an eternal being, but we have to add it to our profile in our God hunt. God always was, and will always be.

The next point we must write on our God hunt whiteboard (at least that's what they do on all the detective shows I've seen) is that God is creative by nature. That indicates a thinking, intelligent being with unlimited resources and power to bring all of creation into being, as described in Genesis. The wonder that is the earth, it's perfect placement just far away enough from the sun for temperatures suitable to sustain life, the amazing liquid called water that is foundational for life, the mathematical order of the universe, all point to a plan, and not a massive random explosion. Richard Feynman, a Nobel Prize winner for quantum electrodynamics, said, "Why nature is mathematical is a mystery. The fact that there are rules at all is a kind of miracle."

Despite how artists have depicted God throughout history, God is spirit without a human body. Human bodies break down, they are mortal. In John 4:24, Jesus says "God is spirit," and in Luke 24:39, Jesus goes on to say, "a spirit does not have flesh and bones as you see that I have."

Someone reading this may have been brought up in a church where God was portrayed as an old man sitting on a throne. God does not have a physical body. God resides in unapproachable light as described in 1 Timothy 6:16, "who alone has immortality, who dwells in unapproachable light, whom no one has ever seen or can see."

The pushback on this is, then why do we refer to God as *he*? If God is not a man, then why is the word *he* prominent throughout the Bible when referring to God? God is a living, thinking being of light, and cannot be called an *it*. The book you're reading is an *it*. The chair you may be sitting in is an *it*. They have no life. They cannot think. God is not an *it*.

Fair enough, but why *he*? Why not *she*? In the Old Testament, God did appear temporarily in human form, three times as a man and four times as an angel. The culture of the nations in the Old Testament was of male dominance, and women were considered property. I'm not saying that God couldn't appear as a woman. After all, God spoke to Moses as a burning bush. Perhaps it was the timing in history that set the pronoun gender choice we use today.

The greatest appearance of God, of course, was Christ in Jesus. "And the Word became flesh and dwelt among us" (John 1:14). The *man* Jesus was and is God incarnate.

God is not limited by time or space as we humans are in our physical bodies. With no restraints of time, God can be with each one of us simultaneously, so God is ever present in each one of our lives. God is omnipresent.

By nature, God is approachable and knowable. God welcomes us into a relationship without formality and without religion. It's a bit strange at first to talk to someone who you can't see, someone who may or may not give you an audible answer, but nonetheless hears your prayers. God wants us to be close to him.

Does this really happen? The Bible is full of stories and testimonies of people who *felt* God's presence or *heard* God's call, but what about today? Do people who talk to God get answers? Absolutely, and that is why the Christian story has survived and thrived over 2000 years. Think about it. Are you going to invest your time and money in something that traditionally has given no returns and is basically a dead horse?

If lives do not change, if the quality of life doesn't improve by believing in God, then why bother? The evidence is to the contrary. Millions of people have testified that belief in and listening to the living God has made an incredible change for the better in their lives on earth. So we need to add to God's profile the testimonies of millions of people over thousands of years. They are God's character witnesses.

God is often referred to as our Heavenly Father, and I would like to use the image of father to better explain God's nature and attributes. I know that for some the word father doesn't have a positive feeling. Perhaps you are one of the lucky ones who had a wonderful father growing up, but for many, the father-child relationship was one of pain and regrets. If your relationship with your father was one of hurt and strife, I ask you to put those feeling aside and imagine the perfect father, because that is what God is to us all.

The perfect father would love us, and love us unconditionally. No matter how bad our screwups, the perfect father's love would not waiver or diminish. He would continue to love us no matter how many times we rejected his parenting, no matter how many times we rejected him.

The perfect father would be fair and just, and because of his love for us, often need to give us an occasional attitude adjustment. His justice would be impartial, because the perfect father would be wise and never make a mistake. In those times of what we would perceive as punishment, the perfect father would show mercy and be gracious in not giving us the whupping we probably deserved.

The perfect father would be our protector, our teacher, and our director in the part we act in this play called life, pushing us to bring out only the best in our character to grow into the vision he has for us.

God is our perfect father. He is by nature loving. He *is* love. God is just, wise, and merciful. He is our creator and sustainer, our protector and director. God has a vision for each of us and wants us to be in relationship with him.

There is so very much more to know about the nature of God, but I close with just this final point. God is our friend. This may seem radically distant from the father you knew, but the perfect father would be our friend. I am blessed to say that even though I am far from being a perfect father, I have this duality with my adult sons. I will always be their father and that relationship is a constant, but I now have the joy of being their friend.

While I still offer parenting advice and fatherly love, I have a freedom to love them as friends, sharing life's adventure on a more leveled playing field. At times my sons are like the brothers I never had in my only-child world, and that is the icing on the cake of parenthood.

God is our father, and God is our friend. God will always be the constant loving parent to us, but also calls us to be as close to him as a close friend can be. Close friends open their hearts to each other in sincerity and honesty. Close friends are always at the ready for each other. Close friendships are sustained by unshakeable love.

Jesus said to his disciples in John 15:15, "No longer do I call you servants, for the servant does not know what his master is doing: but I have called you friends, for all that I have heard from my Father I have made known to you."

Imagine that God in the person of Jesus is calling *you* his friend. That's a far cry from the distant, mean, and grumpy God that so many people grew up learning about. If that was your upbringing and teaching about God, perhaps it's time to rethink the possibility that God is truly the best friend anyone could pray for, the best friend anyone can pray to.

Believing in Jesus

The Christian story tell us that God is the Trinity, one God in three persons. The doctrine of the Trinity states that God is Father, Son, and Holy Spirit. The Apostle John wrote "In the beginning was the Word, and the Word was with God, and the Word was God" (John1:1).

If we replace "Word" with "Son," I believe it brings to light a clearer meaning of the relationship of Father and Son. In the beginning was the Son, and the Son was with God, and the Son was God.

Now please don't turn the page recoiling from the depth of thinking we're trying to reach. Theologians don't call this an "ineffable mystery" for nothing. This is tough thinking that merits our time.

Christians believe that God the Son came to earth in the man Jesus. Jesus was called the Christ or anointed one. He was and is the God Man, but before God came to earth in the man Jesus, Christ made several bodily appearances in the Old Testament. So if Christ could come to earth and materialize in bodily form at his will, why did he need to be born in a human body as Jesus? What's the greater story behind this?

God became man to live with us, to teach us, to model for us and to die for us, and come back to life in the resurrection. God became man, "to seek and to save the lost" (Luke 19:10). God is spirit and invisible. God in Jesus is visible and touchable. It's easier for the human psyche to understand things experienced through the human senses. Jesus the Christ was a real person. He was born to a human mother. He probably played with other children. He traveled with his mother and father. He laughed and cried. He felt hunger and pain, and in all his humanness, he showed wisdom and grace, because he was and still is the Christ.

Historically, there is no doubt that there was a man named Jesus. The New Testament contains hundreds of references to Jesus Christ. Paul's writings are accepted by both Christian and non-Christian scholars to be authentic writings of Paul, who wrote them between AD 50 and 63. Jesus was crucified in AD 33.

Beyond the evidence found in the Bible, there are accounts in Roman writings of the existence of Jesus. The first-century Roman Tacitus wrote about a man named Jesus who lived during the first century. The famous Jewish historian Flavius Josephus refers to James as "the brother of Jesus, who was called Christ."

The most compelling proof of Jesus's existence is the very fact that thousands of first-century Christians were willing to be martyred for their belief that Jesus was Christ and rose from death. They saw their leader nailed to a cross. They watched him die. At that point, it would have been easy to say, "Well, that was an amazing three years of walking with him, but I guess it's over. I'm going back to fishing."

The reason they didn't scatter and go back to their pre-Jesus life was because Jesus did indeed rise and live with them again for a season. Jesus appeared to hundreds after his resurrection.

Then there's the story of Saul of Tarsus. He was highly educated in the Jewish faith. He saw Christianity as a threat to the faith he knew and loved, and made it his goal to capture Christians, bring them to trial and execute them. On his way to Damascus, the risen Jesus appeared to him in a blinding light.

As I was on my way and drew near to Damascus, about noon a great light from heaven suddenly shone around me. And I fell to the ground and heard a voice saying to me, Saul, Saul why are you persecuting me? And I answered, 'Who are you, Lord?' And he said to me, 'I am Jesus of Nazareth, who you are persecuting.' Now those who were with me saw the light but did not understand the voice of the one who was speaking to me. And I said, 'What shall I do, Lord?' And the Lord said to me, 'Rise, and go into Damascus, and there you will be told all that is appointed for you to do' (Acts 22: 6–10).

Saul, who had the Latin name Paul, grew up in a strict Pharisee environment. A Pharisee strictly observed the traditional and written law in the Jewish religion. Paul was zealous for his faith to the point of being a terrorist to the Christian community. He was a rising star in the nation of Israel, yet he made a complete course change and became a champion for Christ. He wrote 14 of the 27 books in the New Testament. He planted churches all through the Mediterranean area. He was beaten several times for preaching the gospel of Jesus. He was cursed and rejected by the people of the Jewish faith he once defended. He was wrongfully imprisoned with no damning evidence, and later killed.

Why would anyone who had status, position in the community, on the fast track to be a religious leader, throw that all away, unless there was a conversion on the road to Damascus, and Jesus changed his heart? Christ, who is timeless, has been changing hearts from the beginning of time. Once Christ grabs your heart, you are willing to take rejection from man, knowing that you belong to and serve the living God.

There are agnostics and atheists who will acknowledge that historically there was a man Jesus, but think of him only as a philosopher or even a magician. Other nonbelievers will argue that there never was a man named Jesus, despite the cross-referencing of history from varied sources. Some arguments against the existence of Jesus are well-crafted, peppered with just enough history to make the fiction appear to be authentic, much like Dan Brown novels, which, by the way, I do enjoy.

If there wasn't a man named Jesus or any God incarnate person, then why is humanity still talking about and debating him? There *is* historical evidence for all the Roman emperors that lived before and after Jesus, but unless you're a history buff, Caesar's name is rarely mentioned, unless you're calling a large dog named Caesar.

The students of history who dismiss Jesus should broaden their research to account for the rippling effect this "nonexistent person" had on history itself.

Take a deeper examination what the world was like before Christ (BC) and after Christ (AD). There was a paradigm shift in world thinking.

In his book *Who is this Man?*, John Ortberg draws a comparative picture of life before Christ and after. The world before Jesus was one where women were considered property. Jesus included women in his ministry and broke down the gender barrier. The world before Jesus valued power, status, and riches. Jesus empowered the poor and began changing social classes. Babies were often discarded onto a dung pile if they were deformed or not the preferred gender of male. Jesus said, "Let the little children come to me."

No world leader has had a greater effect on changing the course of history. This man Jesus held no position, didn't own property, had no money, and pushed back on what was culturally accepted at the time. It would make greater sense for someone with position and power and money to influence the world as he did, but all the power and wealth of the Roman Empire would fade away while the movement of following Jesus grew exponentially.

My writings are an appeal to your logic and thinking to turn towards something that only your heart will tell you is true. I pray that the stage is set for a time when you open your mind and heart to the reality and relationship in Christ Jesus.

Believing in the Holy Spirit

In preceding chapters I have discussed God as Father and God as Son. The third person in the Holy Trinity (one God in three persons) is the Holy Spirit. While it is mathematically correct to think of $1+1+1=3$, it is also mathematical truth that $1\times1\times1=1$. There is one God of three distinct persons. They are interconnected and yet distinctive.

It would be foolish of anyone to stare at the sun. One can't look directly at the sun without the risk of permanent eye damage or even blindness, because of the unseen ultraviolet sunlight that continues to bombard the earth. The temptation to stare towards the heavens increases during a solar eclipse. A solar eclipse occurs when the moon passes between the sun and earth and blocks the sun's light as seen from earth. With the proper eye protection, the proper lenses, a person can watch as the world goes dark for a few minutes. The warming rays of the sun are blocked and the temperature may drop, especially during a total eclipse, but the ultraviolet radiation continues to make its way to the earth.

The sun is basically a continuous thermonuclear explosion that no living thing on this earth can look at or be close to without being destroyed. God, who created the sun and stars, is infinitely more powerful than the total collection of all stars. He dwells in unapproachable light.

God *is* approachable and knowable as the person of Jesus. Much like the special eyeglasses to watch a solar eclipse, Jesus is the proper lens through which we can experience the amazing majesty of God. In John 10:30, Jesus said, "I and the Father are one." In John 12:45, Jesus reiterates, "And whoever sees me sees him who sent me."

In this solar eclipse analogy, the Holy Spirit can be compared to the ultraviolet radiation that consistently showers the earth with life-giving warmth and energy. It affects nearly all living things on earth. The Holy Spirit constantly showers believers and nonbelievers with God's personal presence.

No analogy can fully convey the mystery of a triune God, but let's entertain the idea of a power plant. A power plant's function is to *create* electricity. The electricity created is then delivered to customers via power lines, but not before the high voltage electricity (400,000 to 750,000 volts) is reduced to a lower voltage (100 to 250 volts) via a *transformer.* If you were to try to power your home's appliances with high voltage electricity they would simply explode. Your toaster would be toast.

God the Son *transforms* the amazing power of God the Father, the *creator,* to power us with the perfect amount of God's life force and sustaining love and grace. I now find myself venturing into a deeper conversation of Son and Father that this analogy cannot do justice to, but allow me to add this. The Son who is Christ Jesus does far more than channel God's grace and love to us. Jesus in not only a transformer, but also a circuit breaker.

A circuit breaker is designed to interrupt current flow after a fault is detected. In our humanness, and because of our actions, we produce a current of wrong choices and bad actions (call it sin) that runs counter to the flow of love coming from God. This power surge that we create is negative to God's positive. Jesus breaks the upward surge from this broken world and interrupts the flow because of our fault.

How does the Holy Spirit fit in to this analogy? Think power lines. Without a way of delivery, a connection, the electricity generated by the power plant, then converted by the transformer, would be of no use to us because of a lack of delivery.

The Holy Spirit is our connection. If we think of God the Father as the initiator and creator, and God the Son as mediator, director, and transformer, we can think of the Holy Spirit as the actuator and deliverer. The Holy Spirit has been described as God's personal presence, his energy and breath, the inspiration that empowers people, our guide.

The Holy Spirit guides us in the whispered ideas outside of our own thinking as seen in the divinely inspired scriptures of the Bible, penned by men but written by God though the Holy Spirit.

The Holy Spirit is our comforter in times of trouble. Think of a time when sorrow was drowning you, but a wave of peace washed over you and lifted your spirits. That may have been a time when God's peace was infused into you through the Holy Spirit, the peace that surpasses all understanding.

The Holy Spirit coaches and prompts us. Conscience is defined as an inner prompting to do good or evil. God's blueprint when creating us was to have a call center for inner awareness, a place in our being to help us discern what is right and wrong. The Holy Spirit mans that call center in those who believe in God. I can *let my conscience be my guide* when I listen to and follow the advice and promptings of the Holy Spirit.

In the final hours before his crucifixion, Jesus reassured his disciples in John 14 starting at verse 15. "If you love me, you will keep my commandments. And I will ask the Father, and he will give you another Helper, to be with you forever."

Jesus speaks of the Holy Spirit again in verse 26. "But the Helper, the Holy Spirit whom the Father will send in my name, he will teach you all things and bring to your remembrance all that I have said to you."

Jesus's promise was fulfilled on the day of Pentecost as told in the Book of Acts chapter 2. "When the day of Pentecost arrived, they were all together in one place. And suddenly there came from heaven a sound like a mighty rushing wind, and it filled the entire house where they were sitting. And divided tongues as of fire appeared to them and rested on each one of them. And they were filled with the Holy Spirit and began to speak in other tongues as the Spirit gave them utterance."

I have not felt a rushing wind or fire resting upon me, nor do I believe that the Holy Spirit always manifests in such a dramatic way. I have felt an unseen push in the right direction. I have heard a small whisper in my mind teaching me and inspiring me. I cannot take full authorship of this book.

There is something outside of me, outside of my psyche, my human self, that influences me, teaches me, guides me, and guards me, and I believe that is the Holy Spirit. I believe that the more I open myself to acceptance of this God-presence in my life, the more my life will be on course to become the vision that God dreamed for me long before my birth at the beginning of time.

Right Game, Wrong Team

I am, by no means, a sports aficionado. I can't quote stats or sports facts, but I do enjoy watching a well-played game. I think any sports fan would agree that the best game is a well-played game, when the plan all comes together. Even if the home team doesn't win, there is still enjoyment watching when at least they've kept it close and stayed in the game. It's the love of the game that keeps stadium seats filled, even when the home team is hurting. Tailgate parties before and after are a plus as well, so I'm told.

There are fans known as diehards. They would never consider rooting for another team, even if their team is performing badly. There are fans who jump from team to team, season to season, searching for that golden team to cheer for. And then there are the fans that completely walk away from the game. They have been disenchanted for too long and they are tired of the whole thing, the hoping, the cheering, ticket prices, the game itself. They check out and turn their back on something that at one time made sense.

What kind of church fan are you? Are you a diehard for your church? It may be that you are blessed, as I am, to belong to a church that has propelled you forward into a closer relationship with Christ. It may be that you are a diehard fan of a church that has a long tradition and history, and you find comfort in the community of believers. Whatever your reasons, you are a committed diehard to your church.

There are those that set up camp in a church for a season, but when the pastor preaches a sermon they don't like, or the band plays a song that's too rockin', they pack up and find a new church. Now don't get me wrong. If your church is not nourishing you in your spiritual growth, then it is your obligation to find a church home that fits. I'm addressing, what our pastor calls RV Christians, who move around too much without forming friendships in a community. The right community is essential for spiritual growth. It doesn't always happen overnight.

And then there are the church fans who have checked out. They have come to a point where church seems irrelevant, incapable of answering their questions or meeting their needs. Perhaps it was a hurtful word. Perhaps it was an expectation that wasn't met. Whatever the reason, the result is that they have checked out and turned their back on something that at one time made sense.

If this is striking a chord with you, please consider this. You were playing the right game, but just on the wrong team. When church is done right, you grow in the knowledge and love of God. When church is done wrong, people get disenchanted, confused, more broken than they are, and hurt.

If you were to go out to dinner and experience a bad meal, would you stop going out to eat, or would you find a restaurant to your liking? It would be folly to categorize every restaurant as bad because of one disappointing meal in one restaurant.

If you have turned your back on church, would you consider turning around? Give church one more chance. In the right community you will grow, you will learn, you will change for only the better. Perhaps you have heard that life is a team sport. We are meant to live in community. We need each other just "as iron sharpens iron, so one person sharpens another" (Proverbs 27:17).

Christianity is also a team sport. We need each other for encouragement. "And let us consider how to stir up one another to love and good works, not neglecting to meet together, as is the habit of some, but encouraging one another, and all the more as you see the Day drawing near" (Hebrews 10:24)

When playing on the right team, the game is exhilarating.

Good Fences

I remember the story of an elementary school in rural America. At recess, the children would gleefully run and play in the meadows and woods behind the school building. There had been talk of a major highway that would cut through the backside of the school property, and it was only a matter of time until it came to pass.

Teachers and administrators noticed a change in the play of the children. They didn't run through the meadows and certainly not through the woods that were now separated from the school by a highway. They gathered closer to the school building. Their world had become smaller.

Eventually a fence was installed around the school property to ensure that children would not wander onto the highway. An interesting thing happened. Now with the fence installed, the children reclaimed the meadows. They felt at ease running up to the fence, which ran parallel to the highway. They found an odd reassurance in the safety of the fence. The fence defined their world at recess.

Nonbelievers have said that following Christ means you must give up things you enjoy, stop having fun, and live a stoic and boring life. Their argument is that God will take away all the good stuff, and they're not sure that they want to surrender to that.

Much like the fences that gave the elementary children freedom to run and play again, trusting and believing in God gives us boundaries that are good for life. There is no loss in coming to God, only gain. True, you may have to give up old habits, bad habits, which are hindering you from experiencing a more fulfilled life.

I have friends who are alcoholics many years sober. They all agree that when they became sober, their friends changed, not because *they* left the friendship, but because their friends found no common ground beyond the shared love of alcohol. Do my friends regret losing those past friends? If there is any regret, it is surpassed with the joy of finding new friends of like mind. So, yes, there will be things that change in your life, but they will be good changes.

Now the pushback on that is when you see a nonbeliever who seems quite happy, successful, compassionate, and loving. Christians don't have the patent to these attributes by the way. There are many agnostics or atheists who are wonderful marriage partners, parents, and friends. They give back to the community. They rejoice in humanity and cry for inhumanity. They live a godly life without believing in God.

So what is there to gain within the fences of Christianity? The difference between the believers' fenced lives and the nonbelievers' lives is that those who believe in Christ also have a gatekeeper on watch all the time.

Jesus would commonly use analogies to drive home his point, and because of the culture at the time, the stories would often be agricultural in theme. In John 10, Jesus talks about being a gatekeeper. A shepherd in that time would gather his sheep into the fenced area and stand guard at the entrance or gate, and often sleep in the gate. Jesus says in John 10:7, "Truly, truly, I say to you, I am the door of the sheep. All who came before me are thieves and robbers, but the sheep did not listen to them. I am the door. If anyone enters by me, he will be saved and will go in and out and find pasture."

Jesus is reassuring that those who he calls his own are protected and guided. It's great imagery to believe that in this world we live in, where danger seems to be lurking around the next corner, where inhumanity is the lead story on the evening news, where the pace of life diminishes the peace of life, we have a shepherd, a gatekeeper, who loves us and only wants the best for us. We have a trusted friend whispering to us, encouraging us, leading us to the better life, to the green pastures that he has built for us.

Sometimes it *is* greener on the other side of the fence.

A Good Foundation

I spent most of my work life as a carpenter on staff at Cleveland Clinic, a world-renowned patient care and medical research facility. I didn't come to the clinic as a carpenter. I started in 1975 in the patient transportation department getting patients to their appointments and tests. I then broke the gender barrier and became the first male EKG technician at the clinic in 1977.

It was in 1979 that the clinic started an apprenticeship program for all the trades: carpentry, painting, machining, plumbing, and electrical. A campus the size of Cleveland Clinic requires a small militia of dedicated tradesmen and tradeswomen to maintain and improve the structure of the facility to ensure the best patient care and safety.

I always enjoyed woodworking, and because the clinic allowed employees to bid on other jobs, I was accepted into the apprentice program. My four-year apprenticeship ended in 1983 when I became a state-certified carpenter-cabinet maker.

The coursework focused on all aspects of carpentry, even those I knew I would never use as an in-house tradesman. It was unlikely that I would ever do residential construction on the campus of the clinic, but I needed to know how to build a home from ground to roof. Our department did do some remodeling, but unless I left the clinic to work in the field, I wouldn't put to use the knowledge I learned about commercial building.

One important takeaway that doesn't require a state-certified carpenter to tell you is that having a good foundation is essential to a successful project. The weekend do-it-your-selfers building a backyard deck know that holes must be dug deep enough and usually filled with a concrete mix to support the posts that will carry the weight of the deck. Success depends on the foundation.

In Luke 6:47–49, Jesus is speaking to a great multitude of people with his disciples by his side. He says,

> Everyone who comes to me and hears my words and does them, I will show you what he is like: he is like a man building a house, who dug deep and laid the foundation on the rock. And when a flood arose, the stream broke against that house and could not shake it, because it had been well built. But the one who hears and does not do them is like a man who built a house on the ground without a foundation. When the stream broke against it, immediately it fell, and the ruin of that house was great.

People talk about building a good life for themselves, but so much of the success of that is based on the foundation they were given when young. Now having said that, it doesn't mean that a person who had a troubled childhood can't build a great happy ending. And it doesn't mean that the person who had the perfect family and the perfect life can't derail. The solid and the shaky both have their challenges.

The beauty of a foundation in Christ is that it can be built at any time during the construction of a life. Just as a sinking concrete pad can be shored up by pumping more concrete beneath it, so it is with a life in Christ. If you were built on a bad and troubled foundation, Christ can shore you up. If your childhood foundation was great, but you've allowed it to crack and sink, Christ can shore you up. Once someone genuinely asks Christ to be the foundation for the rest of their life, a new and beautiful life can be built, but it requires work and dedication.

In 1 Corinthians, Paul is writing to the church of Corinth. The people, the new believers of Jesus, were fighting among themselves with disagreements and dissensions. They were all given a new foundation in Christ, but were at odds as to how to build upon it.

Paul, who planted the church in Corinth, writes in 1 Corinthians 3:10–11, "According to the grace of God given to me, like a skilled master builder, I laid a foundation, and someone else is building upon it. Let each one take care how he builds upon it. For no one can lay a foundation other than that which is laid, which is Jesus Christ."

Paul goes on to talk about the choice of building materials in 1 Corinthians 3:12, "Now if any one builds on the foundation with gold, silver, precious stones, wood, hay, straw—each one's work will become manifest, for the Day will disclose it, because it will be revealed by fire, and the fire will test what sort of work each one has done."

It's obvious that if you were to build a house with gold, silver, and precious stones, it will definitely have a better chance of standing up against the storms of life, as opposed to a house made of wood, straw, and hay. The childhood story of "The Three Little Pigs" plays this out with one pig having the foresight to build out of bricks rather than straw and sticks, saving everyone's bacon. But I digress!

Receiving a new foundation in Christ is just the starting point in building a new life in Christ. Building requires planning, and right choices, and commitment. When my sons reached the teenage years, I told them that their mother and I had given them the best foundation that we could. They were now the architects of the rest of their lives. It was, and still is, up to them to make the best decisions to build a good life. As far as my role now, I feel like a consultant. I like to keep my hand in the building process.

It's reassuring to know that our Heavenly Father still has his hand in ours.

Masterpiece

I am a product of the 1950s, formed in the simplicity of what a young boy could do for fun. There were no video games, no Internet, no Laser Tag, nothing to resemble what we would call high tech today. An online experience was when you called a friend on your parents' rotary phone (look it up young people) to make plans to play somewhere, usually outside. I can still hear my parents bellow, "Keep it short. Someone might be trying to call."

The toys I had were simple but stimulating. My baseball glove and bat were always at the ready for a pickup game with friends. On rainy days I would turn to Lincoln Logs or my Erector Set, which helped develop creativity and thinking. One joy that I could immerse myself in was paint by numbers.

The concept was great. Your paint-by-numbers kit would have all the paints, brushes, and pictures to entertain a young artist. The scenes were sketched out on the paper with printed numbers that would correlate with a certain bottle and color of paint. If the color blue was number one, you would find all the number ones on your paper and paint them in. One by one, color by color, the painting would take form, the picture would come alive, and the masterpiece soon found a place of honor on the refrigerator. I rejoice now in reporting that the paint-by-numbers concept is alive and well and living on Amazon, stocked with masterpieces just waiting to be finished.

I want to speak about another masterpiece. You. And me. I believe that God has a vision of what each one of us can grow to be when all the numbers are filled in. We are each given a sketch of the vision God has for us. He has arranged all the needed supplies, the different array of colors and textures of paint, the size of the canvas.

God begins by filling in some of the numbers, then hands us the brush. If we listen carefully, we can hear God whisper when we color outside the lines. If we turn a deaf ear, our painting starts to resemble something wholly other than the sketch of the vision.

Some have strayed so far from the numbered lines that God white-washes the canvas and gives us a redo. God's vision for that soul bleeds through the white on the canvas. This second chance is a blessing, a new start with the first brush stroke.

When painting your life story, allow God's hand to guide yours. Turn to the Master. He still sees the masterpiece in you.

Checklist

I am one who counts on making lists to keep me focused on things that I want to accomplish. I tell myself that it has nothing to do with forgetfulness or the possible early signs of senility, but everything to do with the busyness of my life. After all, for the driven business person, it's not uncommon to have a daily planner or a weekly calendar, or even a secretary to keep them on the right path for success. And while I am no longer in the work arena, I certainly have important goals and responsibilities, that may, and often do, include an afternoon nap. Actually, I don't need to put "nap" on the list. My body usually overrides the scheduled event for the day and demands a quick coma.

My time in retirement need not be scrutinized minute by minute, but I find help in at least charting out the activities I want to accomplish for one day at a time, especially those listed on the honey-do list left carefully positioned by my wife on our island counter in the kitchen. I do get to that list, perhaps not as quickly as she envisions, but again, I'm on retirement time.

Another reason for the hard-copy list is the ever failing mental note. Again, I maintain that it's the sheer volume of activities and ideas floating in my head that prevents making a mental note a success. Pen to paper works best for me.

There is great satisfaction when I cross off an item on my list of things to do, even though the formula seems to be cross off one, add two.

Checklists are indeed a valuable tool for getting things accomplished and keeping appointments, but not so good when it comes to our faith. There lies the pitfall of being a checklist Christian. A checklist Christian has a preconceived notion that as long as he or she does a certain list of rituals or duties, then he or she is "right with the Lord." Attend church. Check. Listen to the sermon. Check. Drop a check in the offering plate. Double check.

Sometimes we are fooled into believing that being busy at church is being close to God. There's nothing wrong, and actually everything right, with volunteering and doing good works for the church and for God's kingdom. That is what we are called to do as followers of Christ. Hebrews 13:16 says, "Do not neglect to do good and to share what you have, for such sacrifices are pleasing to God."

There's no question that doing good is part of the Christian walk. The underlying question asks, is the good you are doing from the heart, or just part of a checklist relationship? The misplaced belief is that because you do good things and works, you somehow gain a closer relationship with God, as though you can earn favor.

Ephesians 2:8–9 says, "For by grace you have been saved through faith. And this is not your own doing; it is the gift of God, not a result of works, so that no one may boast."

The nation of Israel in the Old Testament was formed and cultivated by the customs and rituals found in the writings of Moses. The Hebrews had lost their culture, having been enslaved for over 400 years in Egypt. During the Exodus, forming new traditions and laws was paramount to establishing the nation of Israel. The book of Deuteronomy is the recounting of the necessary checklist for the Jewish nation to survive. However, the laws created a culture, but that didn't necessarily make them spiritual. Laws don't make you holy. They make you a good citizen.

Fast forward to the time of Jesus. He particularly targeted the high priest and Pharisees for their lack of spirituality. They were faithful keepers of the law, but were so blinded by their intent to keep the laws and traditions on their checklist of faith that they completely missed the living Christ in the man Jesus.

If we were to compare the checklist of today's believer, with that of today's nonbeliever, we would find some same line items. Both can help the poor. You don't have to profess to have a belief in God to feel compassion for a fellow human. Both can be loving family members, good parents, and law-abiding tax paying citizens.

Checklists don't make a believer a believer. To be a follower of Christ is to spend time with him in prayer and in his word, to emulate his life and teachings, and to open yourself for his direction. Of all the things we could put on our checklist, Jesus told us two of greatest importance.

He said in Matthew 22:37,"Love the Lord your God with all your heart and with all your soul and with all your mind."

Jesus also said in John 13:34, "A new commandment I give to you, that you love one another: just as I have loved you, you also are to love one another."

If you belong to a church family that has traditions and rituals that are dear to you, I am not advocating for you to drop out. Traditions can bring comfort. Rituals can bring order and a sense of direction. But please don't think that just because you keep the traditions and rituals of your faith, you have reached your final destination. Don't be a Pharisee and miss the living Christ. Church should be the calm in this stormy world where you can find guidance and comfort. It should bring you to a personal soul search for Christ. If it stops short of helping to open your heart to God, then it is no more than a social club.

A fifth-grade teacher decided to teach about customs of different faiths, and so she asked her students to bring to class something that is important to their religion. She started going around the room asking students to show the class what they brought. She began with one young boy, and told him to stand up, say his name, tell everyone what his faith was, and show the class what he brought that is important to his faith.

The little boy stood up and began. "My name is Isaac. I am Jewish, and this is a menorah." The teacher thanked the boy as she called upon the girl sitting next to Isaac.

"My name is Mary. I am Catholic, and this is a rosary." Then it was Mikey's turn. He stood up beaming and said, "My name is Mikey. I am United Methodist, and this is a casserole."

Now to my Methodist brothers and sisters, please know that I speak from experience, having attended a Methodist church for more than 25 years, and yes, there is so much more to the faith and our worship of Christ, but you have to admit, we did eat pretty well in our tradition of having food at most church meetings.

Then there's the story of a pastor who was retiring after leading his congregation for over 30 years. During the transition to the new and younger pastor, the senior pastor would sit with the congregation and listen to the new pastor's sermons. After several weeks, a longtime member of the church approached the retiring pastor with harsh concern.

"I'm not sure this new guy is going to work out," he grumbled. The senior pastor asked him why. The church member replied, "He's changing our service. He doesn't go to the side and touch the metal railing like you would do before praying."

The pastor smiled and said, "I touched the railing to discharge the static electricity before I pick up the microphone. The new pastor will do just fine."

Jesus was quite clear in addressing the Pharisees on the subject of traditions, and it should be our caution as well. In Matthew 15:3, Jesus said "And why do you break the commandment of God for the sake of your own tradition?"

Hold fast to the traditions that nurture you in Christ. Enjoy the comfort of your church, but be on the ready, for Christ has been known to pull you out of your comfort zone. The Christian walk is not a Christian sit.

Own Personal Jesus

The flight from Chicago to Cleveland is less than an hour. The flight path takes you over some large suburbs and major cities. On one particular evening, just before sunset, I was resting comfortably in my window seat, gazing out the window, and watching clouds and cities go by. I wondered about the people living in the thousands of homes we flew over. What were their stories? Everyone has a story, but I would never hear them. I pondered how many people were praying at that particular moment in time, and in particular, calling on the name of Jesus. I believe that when I talk to Jesus he hears me, and I tend to overlook the probability that someone else is talking to him at the same moment.

Johnny Cash wrote and recorded a song called "Personal Jesus," and the concept fascinated me. I know we tend to think of Jesus in earth time as one person in one body, which begs the question of how we can have our own personal Jesus with 7.5 billion people on the planet. It'd be quite a wait in line with a few billion people in front of us.

We try to make sense of an infinite idea with a finite mind. God is not limited by time or the physical world. I can't give you the definite answer as to how God sustains everyone on the planet, or how he can hear 7.5 billion people talking at the same time. I wonder if God just freezes everyone else's time to spend time specifically with me. Time is meaningless to the one who is eternal, so maybe he just pauses the world to be *just* with me and my prayers and thoughts. Again, I find myself trying to explain the unexplainable.

What truly matters is that I believe my prayers are heard. I believe your prayers are heard, and I believe they are answered. We may not understand or like the answer, but it remains an answer.

Let time stop from the busyness of your day, sit in the quiet, listen, and know that you indeed have your own personal Jesus.

"Do not be anxious about anything, but in every situation, by prayer and petition, with thanksgiving, present your requests to God. And the peace of God, which transcends all understanding, will guard your hearts and your minds in Christ Jesus." (Philippians 4:6–7)

The Fight Within

Often I have a good talk with myself man to man. Many times it's in the form of a caution or correction. I like to think of those as course changes with only the best intentions for myself, but often I beat myself up for mistakes made. My tone is sometimes harsh and a bit belittling. I would never be as hard on anyone else as I am on myself.

I don't have the copyright for this behavior. It is in the public domain, used freely and abused by many. Why are we so hard on ourselves at times? What causes this critical analysis of self? What is this internal strife?

Paul wrestled with this conflict of soul as well. In Romans 7:15, Paul says

"I do not understand what I do. For what I want to do I do not, but what I hate I do." Later in verse 19, Paul further explains what he is and is not doing. "For I do not the good I want to do, but the evil I do not want to do, this I keep on doing."

Finally in verse 20, Paul reveals what the culprit is. "Now if I do what I do not want to do, it is no longer I who do it, but it is sin living in me that does it." Paul is in the middle of a heated conflict with himself, a conflict of spirit versus flesh. By human nature, we are prone to feed what pleases our physical existence. The spirit self, the real you, is in direct conflict with where the physical you wants to go, and this can be an exhausting fight.

There is a fable about a man who owned two dogs who fought all the time. It seemed as though they were constantly snarling at each other, which grieved the man deeply as he did have a chosen favorite. Finally the man fed the less-favored dog less food and provided more food to his favorite dog. His favorite dog grew in strength and eventually became top dog, the alpha, the boss.

Now before you get yourself all upset, please remember that this is just a fable and not a how-to on dog training. I don't think there is anyone on earth who loves dogs more than me.

The illustration simply offers an answer as to how we start to settle our internal conflict between our body and our spirit. You need to feed the one that you want to have mastery over the other.

Paul gave clear examples of what is of the flesh and what is of the spirit in Galatians starting with verse 19. Let's approach these instructions as though they were body-building exercises, because in reality, they are.

To build you physical body your routine is titled, "Works of the Flesh." That workout includes exercises like "sexual immorality, impurity, sensuality, idolatry, sorcery, enmity, strife, jealousy, fits of anger, rivalries, dissensions, divisions, envy, drunkenness, and orgies" (Galatians 5:19–21).

The other exercise routine offered is to build the spirit and is titled, "Fruit of the Spirit." The exercises proven for success are "love, joy, peace, patience, kindness, goodness, faithfulness, gentleness, self-control" (Galatians 5:22–23).

Two very different approaches for two very different end results. Paul makes the right choice clear in Galatians 5:16–17. "But I say, walk by the Spirit and you will not gratify the desires of the flesh. For the desires of the flesh are against the Spirit, and the desires of the Spirit are against the flesh, for these are opposed to each other, to keep you from doing the things you want to do."

Now does this mean we are meant to live a life without pleasure or appreciation of all the blessings God has given us? Certainly not, but it should be experienced through the lens of what is pleasing to God. God has blessed us with the human experience that allows us to feel things that only humans can. We can *love* our family and friends and find *joy* in the beauty of nature. We have the opportunity to impact this broken world in a positive way through *peace, patience, kindness,* and *goodness.*

And yes it is acceptable to own nice things, drive a nice car, and live in a nice house, as long as those things do not become idols. All that you have is a gift from God whether you realize it or not. Do not leave God's gifts unopened.

We are living the human dream, not dreamt by man, but by the vision that God has for each one of us. Through our *faithfulness* to God, our spirits will grow, and the things of this world will grow strangely dim, as the old hymn says.

Stay healthy in body, but be prepared in spirit by talking with God often, reading his instruction in the Bible, and most importantly, practicing love whenever you can. For on that day when we lay down these weary bones and leave this world behind, we will be greeted in eternity with these word from Matthew 25:23. "Well done good and faithful servant. You have been faithful over a little; I will set you over much. Enter into the joy of your master."

Great Product, Bad Salesman

The first home that my wife Cindy and I owned was a modest bungalow in a suburb of Cleveland called Berea, a good Biblical name if I must say. It seemed palatial, coming from a one-bedroom apartment, and it was a great setting for the early years of our marriage.

Homeowning, as many of you know, requires time, money, and elbow grease. It was at the prospect of having to paint the house that I allowed a siding salesman in for an estimate. I told him that we had plans to go out to dinner with friends, so our time together would be limited. He reassured me that he was only going to measure the house for an estimate and leave a quote for the materials and labor. Seemed reasonable, so I opened my house to him.

He did indeed measure the house, he did indeed come up with a quote, and then he did indeed spend the next 45 minutes sitting at my kitchen table trying to pressure sell me into signing while my dinner guests waited patiently. He was desperate for the sale. He even said, "If I were drowning, would you throw me a rope." I thought to myself, only if I could put a noose on one end, but politely said to him, "If you were drowning I would for sure throw you a rope, but I'm not signing your contract. It is now time for you to leave." As he left, I thought to myself that he was the worst salesman, and no matter how great his product was, I would never give him my business.

Unfortunately there are bad salesmen and saleswomen who ruin the possibility of landing a sale even when the product is free. The product I speak of is the Good News of Christ. Fervent Christians can often turn off more than they turn on all because of their timing and delivery. Perhaps you've been victim to a pushy believer who seems more hell-bent (perhaps in this case more heaven-bent) to get you to sign on immediately if not sooner. They recite their pre-rehearsed script of quoting scripture without pause. They at times seem to be in a monologue rather than a dialogue, and because of the amount of information being thrown at you without a breath, you shut down and tune out. With all good intentions and passion for spreading the gospel, and with a heartfelt love for Christ, they have unwittingly lost a sale.

Please don't blame them for the intense love they have for God. God has done a mighty work in their lives. They are on fire with a passionate love for Christ, and only want to share it. Their timing and approach needs a little help.

Perhaps we can all learn from the world of sales. A good salesman will try to build a relationship with the client before hard selling. They get to know a little about their clients' personalities and needs. This should be true with those of us in the mission field, the Great Commission field of spreading God's word. As Jesus told his disciples to do in Matthew 28:19–20, "Go therefore and make disciples of all nations, baptizing them in the name of the Father and of the Son and of the Holy Spirit, teaching them to observe all that I have commanded you. And behold, I am with you always, to the end of the age."

Be knowledgeable of your product, ready to answer any and all questions, and if there is a question that you can't answer, remember that "I don't know" is an answer that shows your honesty. "Let me look into that" is a great dovetail. Build a friendship before you attempt to build a bridge to Christ.

At the right time, after a relationship has been formed, ears tend to be more open to your message. Before they care how much you know, they want to know how much you care.

And finally, don't lose hope in what appears to be a lost sale. Your time spent may not see an immediate return, but it may allow someone else down the line to close the deal.

Waiting for the Other Shoe to Drop

I have some good and not so good memories of my childhood. I remember living under the cloud of waiting for the other shoe to drop. In case you're not familiar with the phrase, this could describe expecting something bad to happen as a follow-up to an initial bad event. It can also mean expecting something bad to happen when things are relatively good. Either way, it's usually a bad thing.

Having two alcoholic parents, the good and the bad came in unpredictable waves. I lived with cautious optimism that things would be good, but accepted the harsh reality that things were bound to get bad once more, hence the other shoe drops.

Now this isn't a poor-pity-me party, because all in all, I think I turned out pretty good, if I do say so myself, and I do. In fact, as I look back now from a safe and comfortable future of past hopes, I rest in knowing that I am who I am today because of life events big and small, good and bad. That's not rocket science. Life events have a profound role in forming us. We are a culmination of what we've done, who we did it with, and how we let it affect us at the time.

Hard times help us to purify our thinking. Sometimes you need to hit rock bottom before God can rebuild you, but can there be reward in going through these tough times?

Romans 5: 3–4 says, ". . . we rejoice in our sufferings, knowing that suffering produces endurance, and endurance produces character, and character produces hope."

I can safely say that if you are human you will go through hard times, stressful times, times of anger and anguish. These times seem hopeless with no way out. Times like these have been described as "the dark night of the soul." We see them as pain and not as possibilities for growth, and they are indeed sad times.

When I am in a funk (yes, even Mr. Sunshine gets down), I feel useless to those around me, and most importantly, useless to my God. I am not living the vision that God has for me. I want my happy *me* back, the one that can be an influence for good in my family and with my friends. I want to feel useful again. I want to make a positive difference.

So how can anyone in the midst of an emotional low possibly see it as chance for change and growth? How can we rejoice in our sufferings? What possible good will come from this ordeal?

It must start with the knowledge that God uses hard times to enrich our soul and character. God allows these painful times not to destroy us but to strengthen us.

When raising our children, my wife Cindy and I would use the dreaded time-out if one of our sons was misbehaving. It usually required banishing our boy to his room or an appointed chair for a time of reflection and hopefully repentance. There were no electronics in my sons' rooms, so this really was a time out from their contact with the outside world. All they had was themselves and their thoughts.

That's exactly what our Heavenly Father does when our souls are in a dark place. We are in a spiritual time-out, separated but not disconnected from God, to be alone with our own thoughts. It is our time for reflection. It is the time when the soul is most thirsty for God. I'm not speaking about times of mourning at the loss of a loved one. God is close to the brokenhearted. I'm speaking more about those time our suffering is self-inflicted, and we need a course correction.

Isn't it true that in the hardest of times we tend to pray more? When life is going splendidly we are tempted to turn to God less than when life is out of control and we want Jesus to take the wheel. The good prayer life is consistent, with daily conversations with God. If we practice this spiritual discipline, we will be prepared for life at its best and at its worst.

My sons always knew that after their time-out there would be a discussion of what happened and how to avoid it in the future. They would grow in understanding that as long as we all, the whole family, lived according to the agreed upon family morals and rules, the number of time-outs would diminish to be few and far between.

Our Father God has done the exact thing for all of us. He has mapped out a life for us with guidelines and boundaries. If we adhere to these heaven-sent suggestions, we will hopefully have fewer time-outs. That's not to say that those living the Christian life go without suffering. Truth be told, we are bound to see times of trouble and despair, but because of our belief in God's love, we can go through the suffering knowing that we will be better for it on the other side of the dark night of the soul.

There's one more thing my sons knew after the time-out and discussion that came after. There would always be hugs, and the words "I love you."

And so it is with our Heavenly Father.

Body Beautiful

I was a fat kid growing up. No matter how my parents tried to sugar-coat it, when it came down to the truth, I was fat. I can still hear my mom saying motherly encouraging half-truths like, "You're not fat. You're just big boned." or words like "husky." My favorite fairy tale of the overweight state was that I was just "pleasingly plump."

One evening I woke up unable to breath. My parents rushed me into the bathroom, ran steaming hot water into the tub, and had me breath in the steam. Quick thinking on their part allows me to write today. I remember the words of the doctor the next day telling my parents, "You're killing your son with kindness." He was spot on.

You see, my parents' diet plan was this. Eat everything on your plate and you can have as much dessert as you like. And the dinner plate was usually slathered with several starches and a protein, with some over-boiled vegetable. Don't forget the bread.

Please don't judge my parents' judgement. They tried the best they could, knowing what they knew, but I reached 200 pounds in sixth grade. I was quite the catch with no neck and a butch haircut. For those of you who don't know what a butch or crew cut hair style is, also called a flat top, just think of, in today's terms, buzzed sides and back with about an inch of hair on the top held straight up with a product called Butch Wax, which is exactly what it was. Just think, I was using product on my hair back in the early 60s. You trendsetter you.

So to recap the visual, 200 pounds, no neck, and hair standing straight up. Charming! Under the doctor's advice, I needed to lose weight. This wasn't easy, coming from the sugar addiction of having as much dessert as I wanted. I remember one evening asking if I could have some ice cream. Mom and Dad said yes, but only one spoonful. I grabbed the soup ladle.

Fortunately, by seventh grade, and just in time for my interest in the ladies, I did start to slim down a bit, but to this day keeping a healthy weight is a challenge, especially with age and gravity.

There are also the cards that were dealt to me, and all of us, called genetics, which I don't hide behind, but must honestly be aware of to keep my vision for myself real. The quest for a six-pack abdomen, while feasible, is probably not plausible. I know I have a six-pack. It is well protected beneath the layer of Bubble Wrap called fat.

The drive-home point that I'm making is to have an honest acceptance of who you are, and a healthy expectation of who you can be. You can put a Rolls Royce hood ornament on a Ford, but that doesn't make it a Rolls. Each car has been designed and engineered for a specific function. The Rolls Royce is an exquisite luxury car designed for comfort and prestige. Royalty and those who want to feel like royalty own and sometimes drive these beautiful machines. There are things a Ford can do that a Rolls can't, especially if you drive a Ford 150. They were engineered to be work vehicles.

People, like cars, have been engineered at the factory for a specific purpose. The difference in the parallel is that each human on the planet is unique with no assembly-line match. Some of us would have liked to have been born with a sports-car body, sleek, beautiful, and attractive.

Our society's mantra is body beautiful, and we spend millions of dollars on aftermarket parts and paint jobs to try to reengineer who we are, and negate who we were designed to be. There's nothing wrong and actually everything right with wanting to look good, run good, and stay in good repair. It's really an important responsibility to keep our human vehicle in running order for the safety and comfort of the driver, our spirit self, our true being.

We were born into the body we pilot for a specific reason, which is tethered to the vision God has for our life and to the gifts that he gave us. Finding comfort and resolve in who we are in body comes with knowing who we are in spirit. We are the driver, not the car.

Drive the vehicle that you have been born in. Celebrate the features of that vehicle, and downplay the limitations. Know that at the beginning of the race, the human race, you were placed in that vehicle for a specific goal and vision, with God-specific gifts to help you maneuver the roads ahead. Take good care of your soul's home until the day you trade it in for an amazing new vehicle. Your spirit, your soul, is your true body beautiful.

Candle in a Hurricane

ight is mentioned several times in the Bible. In John 8:12, Jesus said, "I am the light of the world. Whoever follows me will never walk in darkness, but will have the light of life."

Later in John 9:5, Jesus says, "While I am in the world, I am the light of the world." The greeting card writers might say that he is a beacon of hope, a lighthouse on a foggy sea. I say the light bulb went on. While Jesus was on the planet before his death, he turned on the light bulbs for many. He taught a new way to approach life. It was a major paradigm shift from the ways of old. He was a model to emulate and a benchmark to strive for. Now *I'm* starting to sound like the greeting card writers. Let's unpack this.

When people are in light, they are out of the dark. We tend to associate more good with light than we do with darkness. Sunlight is so very important to most living things. Just ask anyone who has endured a long, gray winter sky. The sun feeds us energy. We are energized. There are reasons the suicide rate is higher in cloudy cities.

But is this light that Jesus refers to an actual light? I don't discount the experiences of visions of bright light, or the healing warmth that people will give testimony to, but in this instance I think Jesus is talking about a path, a way of living by choosing light over darkness.

Jesus truly gave us a model of how to live a life walking in the light with compassion, truth, and unconditional love, steadfast and not swayed by other human emotion. He was connected to everyone around him, even when those around him chose to be disconnected. He was focused. He was true to his purpose and knew his purpose.

He left us with this commission found in Matthew 5:14–16, "You are the light of the world. A city on a hill cannot be hidden. Neither do people light a lamp and put it under a bowl. Instead they put it on its stand, and it gives light to everyone in the house. In the same way, let your light shine before men, that they may see your good deeds and praise your Father in heaven."

Those are tall marching orders, but Christ isn't calling us to be Christ. Christ is calling us to be Christ-like. Walking in the light is a conscious decision and practice to pattern our life to follow the teachings, the sayings, and the doings of Jesus, so that, with time, we become what we have practiced. At best, in this lifetime, we can only hope to become a cheap knockoff of the living Christ, but I'd rejoice in that.

Now you might be saying to yourself that the challenge of being Christ-like sure sounds like it requires a lot of work and energy. You are being asked to come close to doing the impossible, given the human condition that we all share. Find comfort in knowing that God lived the human condition in Jesus.

So when you are in deep despair at the loss of a loved one, know that Jesus wept at the death of Lazarus, even knowing that he would bring life back to him. When you are angry and lash out at loved ones, know that Jesus rebuked his closest friends. Jesus found joy in the face of a child, as many of us do. When it feels like the world is ready to crucify you, remember the compassion that Jesus gave in his dying on the cross. He said, "Father, forgive them, for they know not what they do" (Luke 23:34).

Most importantly, when you enter a dark place, and we all do, know that it is hard to keep your candle lit in a hurricane. Don't beat yourself up because you have fallen short of being Christ-like. Celebrate in just being able to hold onto the candle in one of life's storms, and have the faith to believe that it will light again.

What's Trending?

No one would ever call me a fashion statement. My clothes are of modest design with the average man's label of manufacture. I never caught the fever of having to wear something for which I paid more for the label than the cloth. By no means am I judging anyone who enjoys finer and more costly attire. God bless you for keeping the economy going.

We have all been witnesses to the hot trend or sales item that is this year's must- have. Nothing says Christmas more than watching news videos of people coming to fisticuffs over a Tickle Me Elmo.

I must confess that I have succumbed to some trend *du jours*. I grew up in an age of bell-bottom pants and paisley shirts, both of which I owned. I wore my hair long to the shoulders (now a distant memory) and sprouted a full beard and moustache. (Everything old is new again.)

I did own a Pet Rock, which was marketing genius. It was a rock in a cardboard box. When thinking back on this memory, I searched online for information on what I believed to be a passing trend from years gone by, but no. The Pet Rock is still anxiously waiting for adoption on Amazon for $19.95 with free shipping. Mine was only $5.00, but I imagine that pedigree pet rocks are getting harder to find.

The description from the website reads as follows: "Pet Rock is the only pet you'll own that you'll never need to feed, walk, bath, groom or neuter! Pre-trained to 'sit' and 'stay' and best of all, your Pet Rock is the only pet that will never run away!" Marketing genius! In fact, according to the website, the Pet Rock was named one of the top ten toy crazes by *Time* magazine. (I hope a baseball and glove is somewhere in that category.) While we still have some carryover trends from the twentieth century, most of them are in the annals of passing crazes, and for some, thank goodness.

There's a story in the book of Acts that speaks of passing fads. In Acts 5 starting with verse 17, Peter and the Apostles were preaching and healing in a part of the temple in Jerusalem called Solomon's Portico. The high priest and the Sadducees of the temple were filled with jealousy, and Peter and the Apostles were arrested and put into the public prison.

The story picks up at Acts 5:19. "But during the night an angel of the Lord opened the prison doors and brought them out, and said, "Go and stand in the temple and speak to the people all the words of this Life."

Verse 21 says, "And when they heard this they entered the temple at daybreak and began to teach." Now of course this did not sit well with the high priest. He had them brought in to admonish them in verse 28 which says, ". . . We strictly charged you not to teach in this name, yet here you have filled Jerusalem with your teachings, and you intend to bring this man's blood upon us."

Peter and the Apostles pushed back saying in verse 29,"We must obey God rather than men." Well, you can imagine this didn't sit well with the priests of the temple. In fact, they wanted to kill the apostles. Verses 34 to 40 explain what happened next.

But a Pharisee in the council named Gamaliel, a teacher of the law held in honor by all the people, stood up and gave orders to put the men outside for a little while. And he said to them, "Men of Israel, take care what you are about to do with these men. For before these day Theudas rose up, claiming to be somebody, and a number of men, about four hundred, joined him. He was killed, and all who followed him were dispersed and came to nothing. After him Judas the Galilean rose up in the days of the census and drew away some of the people after him. He too perished and all who followed him were scattered. So in this present case I tell you, keep away from these and let them alone, for if this plan or this undertaking is of man, it will fail, but if it is of God, you will not be able to overthrow them. You might even be found opposing God.

Gamaliel was an observer of fads and crazes, trends that come and go, movements that start and stop. If it's a man thing it will run its course in time. If it's a God thing, it can't be stopped.

To follow the teachings of Christ was not fashionable in the beginning. It went against the teachings of the Temple and was considered a threat to Rome; yet, despite persecution of the church from its beginnings to modern day, the church has survived and flourished.

Two thousand years of church history has proven that believing in Christ is not a passing fade or craze. It is a way of life that has not and never will go out of fashion.

As far as what happened to Peter and the apostles next, to know as Paul Harvey used to say, ". . . the rest of the story," you know where to find it.

Dichotomy

There's a sweets factory called Campbell's Sweets in my hometown of Cleveland that is the devil to dieters. I, with great intention, walk past the array of chocolate sweets and gourmet cupcakes and head straight to the popcorn, all 20 flavors. I seek out and grab a bag of one particular flavor called Dichotomy. It's a caramel corn coated in delicious cheese. While other popcorn proprietors offer a mixed bag of cheese corn along with caramel corn, Campbell's has infused both flavors onto each kernel. Genius!

The two-in-one concept translates well into our existence on earth. We are spirit beings living in and piloting a human body. The spirit or soul is the eternal self that, as the word implies, never dies, never stops exiting. The body is mortal, built with planned obsolescence. It is meant to break down and eventually fail to function. We die, or at least one half of our dichotomy does.

While on earth we are governed by the laws of nature, such as gravity. Our body has physical needs, such as food, water, and air. I wonder if that was all explained to us at the assignment of our human body. I picture it like a new-car salesperson going over the features of your recent purchase.

(Off in a daydream)

"Alright then, eternal soul soon to be born Mike Misiak, let's go over the features of your new vehicle. First of all and right up front, you should know that once you enter this vehicle, you will not remember that you are an eternal soul. We call this our veil of forgetfulness feature."

I push back and ask why I have to forget who I am.

"Well you see, that's what makes life on earth a great adventure. You will live in search of who you really are."

I ask if all souls come to realize their true nature.

"Oh heavens no! Unfortunately many souls become so enamored with driving their human body that they come to believe that that is all they are. They spend most of their time in physical pleasures and pursuits, 'living in the moment,' I believe is the earthly phrase. And because they have never questioned who they really are, they face the end of their lease with fear."

I tell my earthly body consultant that I'm a bit concerned at the prospect of forgetting who I am.

"Not to worry. Part of the veil of forgetfulness package includes GPS, God Prompting Service. It's a nonstop broadcast of things you need to know and listen to. This is a learned behavior of course, since you won't remember a thing that I have said."

I raise my concern once again.

"Well, let's take a look at your earth visit. I can tell you that you hit the birth lottery because you're going to be born in America. While that is indeed good news, it also poses the challenge of being too well off in your opportunities and comfort, which could cause you to become more grounded in the physical world, so be careful . . . like you'll remember what I said." My earth body consultant chuckles at the humor.

"Your earth parents were chosen to give you the experiences that you need to experience the most. I can see by looking at their life stories that it will be difficult at times. They both have had tough times. Your earth father lost both parents by the time he was in high school and had to go to work. He later joined the army and served in the Philippines in World War II. He will wrestle with alcohol all his life, as will your earth mother."

I ask him to tell me more about my mother.

"She is the only girl of the family with eight brothers. Oh, this is interesting, your grandfather is a bootlegger who runs a small grocery store."

I ask him how this all affects my life on earth.

"Well, you see, your parents have had obstacles and challenges all throughout their lives, but in spite of those obstacles, they are good people, giving people. They will instill in you good values and plant the seed of faith. You'll also develop a sense of humor to laugh when times are anything but funny."

"Will there be other souls that I'm meant to be with?" I ask.

"Oh absolutely. There was a ton of planning that went into your life story. As with all of the millions now on the planet, there are some things staged and choreographed, customized just for you. That includes the people in your life on earth."

"Is it all written in stone then, or do I have some choice in my life?"

"Your life play leaves enough room for improvisation. You are dealt certain cards. It's up to you to play your best hand."

Now feeling very troubled as to the journey ahead of me, I ask him why anyone would want to give up an eternity of living in the heavenly realm. My consultant's mood changes to somber. "You are God's creation, chosen to incarnate and play a particular role in the drama of the universe. As small as your part may seem to you, it is vital to the overall plan. Do not be dismayed or afraid. God will never leave you or desert you."

I feel at peace. I'm ready to go, when the consultant adds one last thing.

"You asked why anyone would leave heaven to live on earth. Christ left this perfect place to live and die in an imperfect world for one reason . . . love. Go and be the love you are called to be."

"For God so loved the world, that he gave his only Son, that whoever believes in him should not perish, but have eternal life. For God did not send his Son into the world to condemn the world, but in order that the world might be saved through him" (John 3:16).

Just for the Day

We didn't vacation as a family when I was growing up. The big yearly thrill for me was when my mom would take me to Cedar Point for the day. Cedar Point is an amusement park on a peninsula near Sandusky, Ohio, on Lake Erie. The park dates back to 1870, when the first bathhouse and other forms of entertainment were built. So it has been attracting tourists for quite some time.

By the time I was a young boy in the late 1950s, Cedar Point had become the Disneyland of the Midwest, with enough rides and attractions to exhaust this preteen on a hot summer's day. Today it boasts being the Roller Coaster Capital of the World and has more ways to spin you, twist you, invert you, and shake you. More ways than my 60-something stomach can handle without nausea and tossing the two snow cones, french fries, and sweet nuts that I foraged while walking between attractions. In fact, get me to the entertainment halls, where I can sit down and watch a show while washing the midway food fare down with a cold one.

Quite the different scenario from the boy of 11 who ran from roller coaster to roller coaster. In fact, if you were able to ride a certain number of roller coasters in an allotted time, the park would give you a T-shirt, or some token. The summer day at Cedar Point was a golden memory. It was *the* day to look forward to as the last bells of school faded away.

As much as I loved being at Cedar Point, I knew it was just for the day, and by evening, those sobering words of "time to go home" would dim ever slightly the day's joy. It was, after all, part of the bargain. We were at Cedar Point just for the day, and while it was amazing with all of the rides, games, and attractions, it was not home.

Much like that 11-year-old boy at an amusement park, we all are just tourists here on planet earth. We fully immerse ourselves in the rides and attractions this planet, and our physical lives, can offer. We embrace our humanness by loving each other. We are in awe of God's creation in nature. We work. We play. We laugh. We cry. We stress. We run the gambit of human emotions. We eat too many snow cones and french fries. We buy too much stuff. At times we overthink and other times we don't think enough. We do great good, and we do great evil. Just what kind of amusement park is this?

We were born to live the human dream, the human experience, but only for a season, just for the day. We are eternal spirits incarnate in human form on the planet for a short time with an end date written in a wishfully distant future. We know those sobering words, "time to go home" will softly call us out of these human bodies. We know that our time on earth will end, and yet, many go fighting and screaming. So why fight it if we know that it is part of the deal, part of the plan to live on earth for a while, then go home? And there it is.

We've forgotten. We have forgotten that we are, indeed, just sojourners, travelers, visitors in a strange place. This is not our home. Our home is eternal, not finite. Our being is eternal in spirit, not finite in the flesh. In case you haven't noticed, and depending on your age when reading this, your body was designed with planned obsolescence.

It's supposed to wear out. Try as we may to maintain, repair, and occasionally have some work done on ourselves, with a lift here and a tuck there topped off with a paint job, the body will fail, and that's all there is to it. That's the genius of the inventor, who offers a great trade-in deal.

I walked quietly out of Cedar Point at day's end in that lifetime ago, passing a crying child not ready to go home. I felt their sorrow, but also remembered thinking that we were, after all, there just for the day.

At life's end, don't cry because it's over, smile because it happened.

Focus

Isn't it true that while we're with our group of friends, especially Bible-based believers or other like-minded people, that the times together are more enjoyable than not. It's when we step outside of our circle of comfortable companions that our opinions and our beliefs are tested, especially by those who are on the opposite end of the spectrum of our views and attitudes. Our thoughts and beliefs are tested with questions and challenges. We, at times, feel an uneasiness in this inquisition. If we are well-prepared and rehearsed in our thoughts and beliefs, we can usually come away unscathed and oftentimes better for the discussion. The outcome is dependent on our focus.

In Matthew 14 starting with verse 22, Jesus tells his disciples to get into the boat and go before him to the other side of the sea. He would join them later after he prayed alone. While sailing across the sea, a storm came up and started battering the boat with the wind against them. Jesus came to them walking on the water.

The disciples became terrified thinking that he was a ghost, but Jesus reassured them that he was who he was. Peter answered him in Matthew 14:28 saying, "Lord, if it is you, command me to come to you on the water." Jesus answered Peter with one word, "Come."

Peter stepped out of the boat and began walking on the water towards Jesus. It was only when Peter took his eyes off of Jesus and turned his focus on the wind that he began to sink. Jesus, of course, reaches out to Peter taking hold of him, saying to him, "O you of little faith, why did you doubt?"

Peter lost his focus. As long as he kept his eyes glued onto Jesus, he was walking on water. When his focus shifted, he was sinking deep.

I have heard the testimonies of people who say that they have lost their faith. Something happened, usually traumatic, like the loss of a child, and they have given up on God. Have they really lost their faith, or have they lost their focus? The loss of a loved one shifts focus to that of grief, anger, and pain, and for the mourning period, that is how it should be, if we are honest with our human emotions. A pastor friend of mine said that you have to lean into the pain to get through it. We are not meant to reside in grief, anger, and pain, but we must live it for a season. It doesn't go away by itself, and as in Peter's case, it can sink us if we focus on the mountain, and not the mover of the mountain.

Mission Trip

hen our two sons were in middle school and high school, they participated in work mission trips arranged by the Methodist church that we belonged to at that time. It wasn't a spontaneous event. There were months of planning that preceded the actual departure date. A work site had to be decided upon and it was usually out of state to add to the excitement of the travels. Transportation had to be secured for all the work campers, as did sleeping and eating arrangements. There was indeed a ton of preparatory work that had to be accomplished before anyone left, but all of that preparation was well invested as lives were changed, not just in those who were receiving the work, but the work campers as well.

I was teaching senior high Sunday school at the time, and it was a delight to hear the stories of how "awesome" an experience it was, and how it felt "awesome" to make a difference in someone's life. "Awesome" was the word of the year.

This memory came back to me because of a comment made at my morning men's prayer group. I'm not sure of the prelude to the talk, but we landed on work missions, and the one gentleman told the story of how much he enjoyed working with the youth. He said that as much as he enjoyed that time in his life, he hasn't felt the passion to go on another mission trip.

Another member in our prayer group encouraged him and told him that every day we are all on a mission trip. It may not be out of state with 50 or so young teens, but we all have a daily mission. It was almost a throw away comment, but I caught it with intrigue.

In our day-to-day lives, we don't have to wait for a well-choreographed work mission trip to make a positive difference. We can be on a daily mission to make the world around us a little better, to be the force for good if we choose.

I've met people who must have had the mission of making my life miserable, because they sure seemed to try their best, and I must sadly admit, at times succeeded. So we must, on a daily basis, decide what our mission is for the next 24 hours. Are we working for good, or are we working to add more hurt in an already hurting world? Are our actions drawing people closer to God, or further away. My pastor once told the congregation in a sermon that if you are a negative and grumpy soul, please don't let anyone know that you are a Christian.

He's right. Perhaps you've heard it before, but you may be the only Bible someone reads. People are watching you. They will intently watch you if you proclaim to follow Christ. Some will try to use your humanness against you. They will point out those times when you are not acting like the Christ you follow. It happens. They will try to catch you in the "Oh, and I thought you were a Christian!" snare to trip you up and defuse your mission. Stay the course. Know your mission.

If you proclaim to be a follower of Christ, then your mission is simple in statement, harder to implement. Simply put, we are to help people connect to God by helping them grow in and know of the beauty of Christ's love. To be successful in this mission, a course of action needs to be decided upon. Just as in the planning of the out-of-state mission trips of my sons' youth, you may have to plan on leaving your present state, your comfort zone.

Just as my sons took with them the necessary tools to get the work done, we too must also be well equipped and prepared to answer the tough questions a seeker will have. Daily time in prayer and diving into the Bible are the exercises that will empower us to be able to answer the tough questions that seekers will have.

Unlike those Methodist mission trips, there is no one specific time in your life, no one-week period set aside to do good works. Ours is a daily mission that often occurs spontaneously. We don't know when the moment will arise when the door is open for a life-changing conversation. Our backpacks must be at the ready. If you bring just one person closer to Christ, your mission is accomplished, and that, my friend, is awesome.

Heavenly Father, when I am given the chance to be your hands and feet in this world, grant me the strength and courage to be a peacemaker and a life changer.

Help me to see what you want me to see. Help me to be what you want me to be.

Buttinsky

Parenting is, without a doubt, an adventure, to say the least. The early years are a recipe of mostly joy and a bit of anticipation, mixed with a dash of anxiety to do the right thing with this young life entrusted to your care. Recipes and portions differ for each family, but the beginning years usually are the time of teaching and growing up together in the new stage of being a family. Everyone grows. Moms and dads grow their twosome into something larger and beyond themselves. It can be an awesome time of wonder.

Life, while at times challenging, seemed simpler when our sons' ages did not end with *teen*. Up until that point, it was understood that Mom and Dad were like benevolent dictators who would listen to their pleas but still have the final word. The teenage years definitely opened a new chapter in parenting.

I believe in their heart of hearts my sons knew that the decisions we made and the values we held were for their absolute best interest. They knew we loved them, but yet there were new waters to test and new limits to push.

Now please don't misinterpret my representation of my sons. They were fine young men then and have grown to be fine adults, of whom I couldn't be prouder. We are best friends beyond the father-son love.

They both have thanked Cindy and me for the kind of parents we were and for the upbringing we gave them.

Mark Twain said this about the teenage years. "When I was a boy of 14, my father was so ignorant I could hardly stand to have the old man around. But when I got to be 21, I was astonished at how much the old man had learned in seven years"

Seems like a happy ending stopping point in the story, but parenting has no end, even when your children are adults, which opens yet another chapter in the unwritten (but I wish I had one) parenting book.

Now having two adult children, I find myself a tad more cautious when choosing moments to offer unsolicited advice. The internal dialogue goes something like this. "I wouldn't do it that way, but he *is* an adult now, so I probably shouldn't say anything."

Other times the internal dialogue is more direct. "He's probably not going to like me giving him advice, but I can't let this go. I love him too much!"

A good father, or a good mother, will always give advice and direction to their child, because that's part of our job description. We never stop loving them. We never stop thinking of them. We always want the very best for them.

A good friend of mine is jokingly called a buttinsky by his adult children for butting in with unsolicited advice or opinions. He's unapologetic and will continue to speak what he believes is best for his children. I believe the same.

Let me tell you about our Heavenly Father, yours and mine. He is a good Father in that is constantly in our lives. He wants to give advice, He wants to give direction, and does so more than we acknowledge. It's not that God has a speaking problem. It's that we have a listening problem, an attention deficit disorder, if you will. We turn a deaf ear to the whispers of the Holy One. We turn a blind eye to the daily signs, those things dismissed as coincidence or luck.

We act like the rebel teenager who strives to carve out a life on their own, ignoring the heartfelt advice of a loving parent. Sometimes, especially when life is going splendidly, we misplace the praise and belief that we have mastered a happy life on our own accord, ignoring the fact that God has sustained us. God is placed on the back burner.

We refocus on God when life takes a wrong turn. Then we question God's intention or place, and often forget that even in the dark days of living there is still a blessing, a plan from God.

When we come to the realization that, as with a loving earth parent, God only wants what is best for us, then and only then will we realize the dependent relationship we are in with our Heavenly Father. Then will we affirm that Father knows best.

"If then, though you are evil, know how to give good gifts to your children, how much more will you Father in heaven give good gifts to those who ask him!"

(Matthew 7:11)

Demons and Dreams

realize the title of this chapter sounds like a racy made-for-TV drama with adventure and seduction. Actually, I just want to talk about a dream with demons in it. Oh, not like the sci-fi demons that you could almost predict will jump out just as the music in the movie builds. There was no predictability for the demons in my dream.

The dream began with me standing with two people, a young woman holding on to my left arm gently with her two hands as though escort. There was a young man holding my right arm in similar position. I didn't feel threatened at first, but something prompted me to ask them, "Do you know Jesus Christ?" I first asked the woman, who snarled and turned her head away. Same reaction from the man. I found some humor in turning to one, then the other, saying "Jesus," and watching them snarl. This was funny. Jesus, snarl, Jesus, snarl. I have to admit I was playing with them, though I realized they meant me harm.

Fast-forward, as dreams will do, and I found myself, this time, with a vicious dog-like creature on each arm clamped down tight. When I said "Jesus," they too would snarl, but tightened their grip. There was no humor dealing with these two. The more I said "Jesus," the more they growled and clamped down until I must have, in my struggle, said "Jesus" enough times for them to let me go.

Again fast-forward to being alone, walking on a highway, knowing I was heading home, but always finding myself lost. No matter how I would recalculate my course, I was always lost and going nowhere. Curious thing was that I never said "Jesus" once.

Well Sigmund Freud, the Austrian neurologist and the father of psychoanalysis, would have had a field day with this dream. Truth be told, he probably would have had a field day with me in general, but he died too soon. His loss.

Let me take a shot at this. Those entities that try to separate us from our God come in different packages. I believe in the existence of evil. I believe there are fallen angels and demonic creatures who will do everything in their power to keep us separated from the light of God. This earth is their realm and they are threatened by those who seek goodness, who seek God.

The first two, the young man and woman, were human to look at. They seemed harmless and were gently nudging me forward to where they wanted to take me. I, in fact, allowed them to get close to me. I initially perceived no harm, no danger. Perhaps they symbolized the *demons,* so to speak, that we bring on ourselves. Just one more drink, one more look at porn, one more cheating time on my spouse. The regrets of losing temper. The angry word that wounds a loved one.

We all have baggage we keep kicking along like a tired suitcase as we wait in the corded off aisles of life for the next person to move along, the next life event to happen.

(Off in a daydream)

"What's in the bag, sir?" I'm asked.

"Oh, just some demons from my past that I can't seem to leave behind"

"Why did you let your guard down?"

"I thought I could handle it. I thought I wouldn't get caught. I thought God wouldn't see."

"Well, we can get rid of that bag if you'd like." the TSA agent (Timely Spirit Advisor) says, "but you have to turn away from the idea of ever doing it again. You have to walk away from the life you knew and the person you were. You'd be turning over a new leaf, so to speak, wiping the slate clean, as long as I'm using worn-out sayings. What do you say?"

"That would be great!" I say. "But what are you going to do with this bag full of demons?"

"We pile them over by that cross over there, and they just disappear."

"Thank you, Jesus!"

"The name is Gabriel. Next in line, please."

The second pair of demons, the vicious dog-like creatures, were the real deal, as real as dreams will go at least. These are the external forces that actually initiate action against you, and are harder to shake. It was more of a struggle to shake them, because they had as much intent to hold on as I had to shake them off. They have a real stake in keeping goodness and light off the planet, because it loosens their hold and control of humanity.

I believe there is a direct correlation to the number of fallen angels and demons on this planet and the number of followers of Jesus. Every time someone comes to Christ, evil is weakened. That's why evil can come cleverly packaged. It has a vested interest in keeping the world away from Christ.

As for the part of my dream where I was wandering highway after highway never finding my way home, that is pretty much self-explanatory. It speaks to the times when I don't partner with Jesus, when I believe that I can handle it on my own. Christ wants to partner with us in all of life's happenings, but often it is a temptation to call upon Jesus only when the task or challenge seems too large. I'm guilty of not including him in the small victories of life, even though I know in my heart of hearts that he is always with me.

This thinking may have been spawned in the early childhood teaching of being a good boy, and nurtured later by society's call to be a self-made man. At any rate, many will think it countercultural to be dependent on someone other than themselves.

Let's change the frame from dependency to partnership. When we acknowledge, when we partner with God, we are then and only then living to our full potential, and growing into the vision that God has planned for us.

As for Sigmund Freud, I can only imagine what he might want to tell me as to my dreams. "No more nachos before bedtime."

Man of the House

It's interesting to watch the societal changes over the decades as reflected on the big screen and the home screen. (Some home theaters are growing large enough to compete with movie houses, so the words "big screen" are subjective.)

After the stock market crash of 1929 heralded in the Great Depression, films out of Hollywood offered escapism by watching Fred Astaire and Ginger Rogers flying through the air in beautifully choreographed dancing marvels. The early 1930s also saw the rise of gangster films, which echoed the desperate anger of the state of poverty, allowing audiences to vent through Edward G. Robinson or James Cagney. (If these names don't ring a bell, bear with me until I get to your decade.)

The National League of Decency (also known as the Catholic League of Decency) was formed in 1933 to basically condemn movies thought to be objectionable from the point of view of the Catholic Church in America. According to my extensive research (alright. . . one article on Wikipedia), "the idea of censorship appealed to the people who thought that the overall good was more important than individual liberties."

Audiences in movie theaters did literally gasp at the last words spoken by Rhett Butler in *Gone with the Wind* as Clark Gable used (yes he did!) the D word. "Frankly, my dear, I don't give a damn!" America, at least in the movie houses, found offense with what we would now consider an accepted exclamation.

The movies of the 1940s began to take more license with subject matter, but the newer medium of television remained reserved in its portrayal of American life through the 1940s and into the 1950s, when I spent time with *Lassie, Sky King, Ozzie & Harriet, I Love Lucy, Leave it to Beaver, Father Knows Best*, and my must- see favorite, *The Twilight Zone.*

There were shows in the 1960s that carried forward the ideology of decency and wholesomeness, including shows like *Andy Griffith, Beverly Hillbillies, Dick Van Dyke, The Brady Bunch*, and *Mister Ed*. Of course my favorite from this decade was *Star Trek.*

By the 1970s television programming started taking more risks, with shows that focused on issues of the day, such as race, politics, and equal rights. *All in the Family* starred Carroll O' Connor, who played Archie Bunker, a blue-collar bigot, and addressed issues that were taboo for television, such as religion, homosexuality, racism, and the Vietnam War.

The Jeffersons, an offshoot from *All in the Family,* depicted a African American family who moved up the socioeconomic ladder and became one of the longest-running sitcoms with a predominantly black cast in the history of American television. Personal favorites from this decade were *MASH* and *Taxi.*

We've got a couple more decades to go, and I promise that this writing *is* going somewhere.

Television in the 1990s really started to break new ground and push boundaries. Quoting from the website classic-tv.com, "The 1990s brought us many breakthrough television shows with story lines that reflected important issues like multiculturalism, sexuality, and other social issues. Sitcoms during this time also showcased a more gritty view of the typical middle class American family compared to the idealized versions previously seen in decades past. Shows like *Roseanne, Married . . . with Children,* and *Family Matters* were big hits that connected with audiences nationwide."

There were groundbreaking dramas like *ER, NYPD Blue, Law and Order,* and *LA Law,* which did not shy away from the hard topics of the time. If pressed to name a few personal favorites, I would say *Cheers, Friends, Frasier, Seinfeld,* and *Drew Carey* would rise to the top. I was not a fan of the gritty view of America then, and I'm still not.

Alright young person reading this, we have finally advanced into your century of television—the 2000s. Actually, we live in a century that transcends mere television. We now have Internet and cable and streaming and satellite. We have smart phones and smart TVs. We can watch the world on a screen that fits in our hand and goes anywhere.

With this technological ease of access, we as a society can view things that can nurture and grow us, or poison and kill us, figuratively and literally. Views beyond censorship or screening can guide our thinking in a positive or negative direction. We have to be intentional in what we watch and what we believe.

Does art imitate life, or does life imitate art? Are the movies and shows we watch an honest depiction of the life we are living, or are we swayed to live life in a way that emulates the videos and broadcasts we watch? Again, we all have to be intentional, selective, and alert with our thinking.

So what was it that started me down this historical narrative of television and film history? While this has been informative and, hopefully for some, a good time spent on memory lane, where is the mind of Misiak taking us?

It all started one morning in a life group that I belong to with a brief comment on how the role of the man in the home has changed. Television shows and even commercials often portray the man of the house as a bit goofy and even incompetent. "Man" is often the punch-line to a joke that has no basis.

Sadly, in portions of our culture, the man has abandoned his responsibilities in parenting and marital relations, and the woman is left with the incredible and often daunting task of raising children alone. This too adds to the negative caricature of what it means to be a man in this society.

The whole unisex movement of the 1960s clouded the meaning of what it is to be a man by promoting the notion that men and women are the same, except for the obvious physical differences. We are not, and I say that with confidence, having negotiated a wonderful marriage since 1976.

If television and movie portrayals of men are getting it wrong, and if the cultural perception of men is misguided, then how does a man know how to be a man? There is no Man 101 course at my local community college, although there is a known textbook on this topic written by the inventor of man. God has a vision for what a man should be and what a woman should be, and he explains it in his book—the Bible.

In his book *Kingdom Man*, Tony Evans states that "The King has given you a rulebook by which you are to govern—by which you are to rule, lead, make decisions, direct, guide, and align your life choices. This rulebook is His Word."

We are in an identity crisis of manhood, because we have become complacent in who or what we allow to mold us as men, and as women. When God created us, man and woman, he did so with an intended vision and purpose for each. He wired us differently and yet compatible to complement each other in celebration of our differences.

We are God's creation. He has scripted a destiny, an endgame for us that we can only fulfill if we play by his Book.

"I appeal to you therefore, brothers, by the mercies of God, to present your bodies as a living sacrifice, holy and acceptable to God, which is your spiritual worship. Do not be conformed to this world, but be transformed by the renewal of your mind, that by testing you may discern what is the will of God, what is good and acceptable and perfect." (Romans 12: 1–2)

Living Water

Seventy-one percent of the earth's surface is covered with water. The human body is composed of mostly water, 50% to 75% depending on your age. We can live without food for several weeks, but without water, our body begins to shut down in just a few days. It is without doubt that we live on a water dependent planet, alive in a water dependent body.

In my youth, the main source of getting a drink of water was usually from the kitchen faucet, and sometimes, on a hot summer's day, from the garden hose in the back. Deep thirst would overlook the slight nuance of rubber-flavored water.

In the twentieth century, bottled water came in the form of luxury imports like Evian or Perrier. Today there are hundreds of brands of water bottled in easy to grab plastic bottles. Millions are sold. Forgive us, Mother Earth.

The choice of water ranges from Hawaiian Natural Artesian Waters, filtered through 13,000 feet of pristine lava rock, to water from a distillery in Pittsburgh. There are flavored waters, carbonated water, and vitamin-enriched waters all for the taking. Add some hops, barley, malt, and yeast, and water becomes the perfect pairing to a double-cheese pizza, but beer is not water. It is beer, a new creation.

So it is with religion. God set before us a simple plan to know him better and grow into a closer relationship with him. God became flesh in the man Jesus, who was all man and all God. Jesus came to change the paradigm from being under the Mosaic Law, with 613 commandments, to just 2, love God and love one another. Jesus did not say to love God and love one another, and come up with a checklist of rituals and duties. His command was as pure and simple as untainted water, but we all have in our human nature the need to make things more demanding than they are.

When we add anything to Christ, we actually take away the pure essence that is Christ. We are adding flavoring to make Christ more palatable to our personal taste. This is not a new problem with religion. Back in the days of the early church, Paul wrote a letter to the newly formed church in Galatia. He wrote to counter those who were teaching that you still had to follow the laws of the Old Testament. They were basically saying that this new way of following Christ was great, but you should really keep some of the old customs and laws.

Paul says in Galatians 2:16, "Yet we know that a person is not justified by works of the law but through faith in Jesus Christ, so we also have believed in Christ Jesus, in order to be justified by faith in Christ and not by works of the law, because by works of the law no one will be justified."

Paul admonished them then to keep additives out of the pure grace of God in Christ Jesus. The same warning applies to today's church. Denominations have created manuals for membership that have lulled people into a shadow religion of what is meant to be a true relationship with Christ. For the most part, the main ingredient of Christ is present, that is true, but the taste of Christ has been tainted by a litany of dos and don'ts that are more about tradition and custom.

Please do not perceive this to be an attack on organized religion. If you are Catholic and love your church, be the best Catholic you can be, but love God first.

If you are Protestant and love your church, be the best Protestant you can be, but always love and please God first. Be careful that the things being asked of you are in no way diluting God's amazing grace in Jesus.

In the new membership classes held at our church, one of the teachers is wise to say something along these lines to the incoming members. "We are delighted that you love our church, but if we as a church don't help you grow to love Christ, then we have failed you." Church is the vehicle. Christ is the ride.

Jesus offers to us today, just as he did to the Samaritan woman at the well, living waters. Jesus told her as recorded in John 4:13, "Everyone who drinks of this water will be thirsty again, but whoever drinks of the water that I will give him will never be thirsty again. The water that I will give him will become in him a spring of water welling up to eternal life."

Don't dilute the love of Christ. Don't add your own flavoring to Christ's living waters. It already is a sweet drink on its own.

Cover the Cross

In my retirement I have enjoyed the luxury of allowing my body clock to tell me when to rise and shine. It's a sweet treat not to have to attack (and I mean that in the physical sense) the 5:20 a.m. alarm that is now a distant memory of my working days. The few days that I do set my alarm for are Tuesdays and Wednesdays, for a 6:30 a.m. Bible and prayer group with six to eight men from my church.

One morning we were discussing Mark 11:15, which is the passage where Jesus entered the Temple and began to drive out those who sold and those who bought in the Temple, and how he overturned the tables of the moneychangers. One of the men in our morning prayer group recalled how in his Catholic days he would ponder if Saturday night bingo was any better or worse than the money changers in the temple. No judgement was passed by our morning brotherhood, but one particular part of his story struck me and stuck with me.

Because they allowed smoking in the fellowship hall, they would cover the crucifix with a blanket or cloth so that smoke would not stain it. The intention of not tarnishing the cross was sensible. The congregation respected and cherished the cross and what it stood for—the amazing sacrifice given for love.

Somehow the symbolism went deeper to me. Was covering Jesus's face a subliminal act of hiding? Have I, personally and figuratively, covered the cross when I thought I was doing something I didn't want Jesus to see, as foolish as that may seem?

Jeremiah 23:24 says, "Can a man hide himself in secret places so that I cannot see him? declares the Lord. Do I not fill heaven and earth? declares the Lord."

There is no hiding. No matter the self-justification for our actions, all we do is known to him. We can cover the cross, but he can see through the smoke and mirrors.

Slow Drift

When our sons were younger we would vacation with my sister-in-law, her husband, and their two children. The cousins got along famously, as we all did. One of our favorite vacations was at an ocean beachfront. We tried to plan the trip every other year. The kids loved the sand and jumping in the waves, and quite frankly, I loved it, too. I'd be in the waves right with them, not only for their safety, but for my own enjoyment.

With age came an acquired amount of independence from Dad, which was fine, but I always kept a watch from my beach chair because of the tides that would move the kids down from our camped-out portion of the beach. They'd look up in amazement when I would yell to them to swim back to our oceanfront stakes. In the midst of all the fun they were having, they didn't notice that they were slowing drifting away from where they should be.

Isn't this true as we try to live out the Christian faith? We start with all good intentions, such as daily Bible reading and prayer time. We regularly attend church, or participate in life groups, but then comes the gentle undercurrent that life's distractions can bring. We might skip a day of reading the Bible, which seems to get easier with every passing day. We might get out of the routine of church or study groups with an intended short-time planned, but slowly it becomes more and more habit as we float further away from where we should be.

People think it's the big mistakes or sins that sink you like a sudden tsunami with quick and devastating results, and that can indeed happen. But it's the slow unnoticeable drift that quietly sneaks up on you that distances you from God. The *Titanic* didn't sink because of a huge hole in the hull. It sank slowly because of a series of gouges that allowed water to seep in and flood the doomed ship.

Hebrews 2:1 says, "Therefore, we must pay much closer attention to what we have heard lest we drift away from it." Not just *closer* attention, but *much closer* attention. We have to be intentional in our focus to be clear on what is lifesaving, as opposed to what is life-taking.

When the busyness of life's demands replaces God time, then we are drifting. When the physical wants and pleasures take center stage and push God into the wings, then we are drifting.

The slow river ride of life can lead to rocky white-water rapids, and sometimes take you over the falls. Stay focused on the landmark of Christ, who waits on the shore. He is our safe harbor. He is the calm in rough waters. Oh, and one other thing, paddle furiously.

The Fork in the Road

No doubt about it. If you're alive and living in this world, you'll be confronted with the need to make decisions. Many are routine and incidental, like the kind of salad dressing your taste buds crave on a particular dinner night out. Most will agree that your choice of Thousand Island over balsamic vinaigrette should have little lasting impact on the eternal happiness in your life, unless of course you have an egg allergy, in which case I highly recommend the vinaigrette.

It is when we are confronted with a truly life-changing decision that our plan of action should be carefully calculated. When we find ourselves at the proverbial fork in the road, life choices become more demanding than salad dressing choices. The rest of our life and afterlife hinges on making the right decision, on choosing the right road.

I'm speaking of the most important fork in the road that anyone will be faced with. Do you consciously and intentionally want to let go of previous life patterns and establish new life disciplines, or do you want to stay on the road of this world?

In his poem "The Road Not Taken," American poet Robert Frost writes about being a traveler coming upon the choice of two roads in the woods. After pondering which one to take, he reflects that his choice of taking the one "less traveled by . . . made all the difference."

You might imagine that the spiritual road choice at the fork in the road is a hard left turn or hard right, going separate ways east and west. Truth is, when you choose the spiritual highway, you'll soon discover that earth's cultural freeway runs in straight parallel. The attractions and distractions that you were often detoured by in your old life's journey are visible and tempting. In fact, as you drive farther, you notice tire marks in the grassy median that divides the two highways, evidence of someone veering back to their old ways. It happens. Sometimes those old habits pull us off course. I can hear my GPS saying, "Recalculating!"

Fortunately, the grassy median allows a course change both ways, as observed in the returning tire marks. If you are committed to reaching your chosen final destination, don't be dismayed when you cave in to old habits and life patterns. Remember that you may be in the driver's seat, but in those rough times on rocky roads, you're not traveling alone.

Country music artist Carrie Underwood wrote and sang a beautiful song with a title that is a fitting prayer when we go off road. "Jesus, take the wheel."

The Man by the Red Velvet Rope

I have never been to one. I have only seen them on television or in the movies, those late-night hot spots that attract trendy and want-to-be-trendy people. It's the kind of nightclub that is *so* popular and is *the* one to be seen at that there is usually a line to get in. To maintain the appropriate amount of revelers inside the club, and to maintain crowd control outside, there stands the man by the red velvet rope.

Now one would think admission into the club is granted by your position in line, but then come the line jumpers, who for some reason are welcome to bypass the line and enter directly. This seems subject to the reasoning of the man by the red velvet rope, and few argue, as he is usually well appointed in dress and muscles. The man by the red velvet rope is most powerful as to who gets in and who doesn't.

There is a man who stands by heavens red velvet rope, a man with all power to welcome you or turn you away, a man who is most powerful. That man is Jesus. The man at the night club may or may not know you. Jesus knows all of us, our hearts and our innermost thoughts.

I can imagine standing in line excited at the hope of getting into heaven. As I stand there, I, in my humanness, look around and try to guess who's getting in and who's not. As the line moves along, I am amazed how wrong I am in my guesses. People who I think would never get in are welcomed immediately, and others who I thought were shoe-ins are turned away.

I imagine overhearing the conversation going something like this as the people at the front of the line plead their case.

"Lord, Lord, did we not prophesy in your name, and cast out demons in your name, and do many mighty works in your name?"

I think to myself that they surely must have a great point there, but then I hear Jesus's response to them.

"I never knew you; depart from me, you workers of lawlessness."

Wow! I thought I had it all figured out. I thought I could bet on who was getting in through the pearly gates and who wasn't. Then I realize the folly of my human comprehension, and at that point I start to squirm with worry. What if *I* have gotten it wrong all of these years? What if in my sincere desire to know Christ I have fallen short and my faith has been nothing more than a shadow religion?

Now my mind is racing. I mean, after all, I was totally wrong in judging who did get in based on *my* judgments of their lifestyle and behaviors. I guess there were things that I didn't know about the person who only Christ would know, who only Christ could forgive.

In all honesty, I can't tell you how my imagining ends. I hope it ends with me hearing the words, "Well done, good and faithful servant. Enter into the joy of your master." Isn't that what we all hope for, to hear the words welcoming us home into eternity? I pray often that my quest to know Jesus personally is genuine and not just lip service. I definitely want to get this right. I pray the same for you. See you in line.

Bookend

Often books on a shelf are held upright by a matching set of bookends. I have two pieces of petrified wood that frame a portion of my collection. Those stone monoliths keep my books erect and in a designated order of topic.

This book began with an invitation to believe the unbelievable, and this final chapter is the matching bookend that asks the same of you. Hopefully the collection of writings between the beginning and end of this book have stirred the curiosity of the unbeliever, and excited the passion of those who believe.

Those still craving science to prove the unbelievable may find interest in the story of Our Lady of Guadalupe. On December 9, 1531, a Mexican peasant named Juan Diego saw a vision of a maiden at a place called the Hill of Tepeyac found in the Villa de Guadalupe. The maiden identified herself as the Virgin Mary as she spoke to Juan in his native language and asked for a church to be built on that site.

Juan Diego went to the archbishop of Mexico City, Fray Juan de Zumarraga, and told him of his encounter and the request to build a church. The archbishop didn't believe him, but Mary appeared to Juan Diego and encouraged him to try again. On December 10, Juan talked once again to the archbishop who instructed Juan to ask the lady for a miraculous sign to prove her identity.

On December 12, 1531, Juan Diego met with Mary, who instructed him to gather flowers from the top of the hill. It was December, and the hillside would normally be barren, but Juan found Castilian roses not native to Mexico blooming there. Mary then placed the flowers in Juan's cloak or tilma.

When Juan opened his cloak in front of the archbishop, the flowers fell to the floor, and on the fabric was the image of Mary, the Virgin of Guadalupe.

If I were to stop here, it reads as a legend or make believe bedtime story. That's where science brings an interesting turn in the story. The tilma, or cloak, is made of agave fiber, which should have a life span of 15 to 30 years. After 500 years it has maintained its integrity, which in itself is miraculous without taking into account that for the first 115 years it was not under glass and subject to candle smoke, humidity, and the human hands of believers. Replicas began to degrade after 15 years.

Between 1785 and 1791, a workman was cleaning the glass case of the tilma when he accidentally spilled a cleaning solution with nitric acid onto the image. This type of chemical spill should have destroyed the image, and yet it was reported that it self-restored over the weeks that followed to show only small stains on the parts of the cloak not imprinted with the image.

In 1921, an activist against the church planted a bomb in a pot of roses and placed it before the image. When the bomb exploded, the glass case remained intact despite other windows being shattered throughout the old basilica. A brass crucifix standing near the tilma's case was bent back and is now preserved at the shrine's museum.

Here is where it really gets interesting. In 1929 the official photographer of the old Basilica of Guadalupe, Alfonso Marcue, photographed the cloak. Upon developing the photograph, much to his amazement, he saw an image of a bearded man reflected in the right eye of the Virgin. This prompted a closer inspection of the cloak, particularly the eyes. The image of the bearded man was indeed in Mary's eye on the cloak. The man was believed to be Juan Diego.

In 1956, noted ophthalmologist Dr. Javier Torroella Buenos declared that the images in Mary's eyes were scientifically accurate according to the Samson-Purkinje effect that states that the human eye reflects what it sees in three images, two right side up and one upside down. This is in correspondence to the curvature of the cornea. There would be absolutely no way that anyone living in 1531 would have the science and knowledge to paint a forgery with this detail.

In 1979, Dr. Jose Tonsman, with the use of digital imagery, magnified the iris of Our Lady's eyes 2,500 times to reveal the reflection of at least 13 people, thought to be Juan Diego, the archbishop, and the other 11 witnesses present when Juan Diego opened his cloak.

The stars on the cloak are the exact configuration of the stars on that December day in 1531, but not viewed from an earth's point of view. When we look up at the evening sky, we view the stars and constellations from our one and only point of view, standing on the earth. Let's say the moon is in the left sky and the big dipper is on the right.

Now, if we could view our earth from beyond the stars, the moon would be on our right and the big dipper on our left. The stars on the cloak are the exact configuration of the stars on December 12, 1531, but a mirror image from what we would see from earth. It was from a heavenly view. The true miracle of Our Lady of Guadalupe is that in the seven years after the first visit by Mary, close to 10 million Mexican natives converted to Christianity. God spoke to them then and is still speaking to us now.

God speaks to us in science. God speaks to us in the mathematical order of the universe. God speaks to us in the beauty of nature. God never stops speaking. If you wait to hear God shout in large miracles, you'll miss his small, daily whispers. God is calling you right now. Listen and believe.

Acknowledgements

Thank you Karen Ellicott for not only proofreading my text and making sure it made sense, but also for the times we spent over coffee when we shared our theology. I appreciate your friendship.

Thanks to the awesome team at BookBaby for content layout and cover design.

Thank you to my brothers and sisters in the faith at Christ Church, the members of the life groups I attend, and of course my Christ Church bandmates.

A very special thank you to my pastor and mentor, Dr. Dave Collings. Your teaching and preaching have made the Bible alive in me. I am closer to Christ because of meeting you. I truly appreciate your friendship.